"The media would have us believe ____
unhealthy, unhappy, and unhinged! Baloney! Msgr.
Rossetti, who is well aware of the struggles of priests,
shows them to be men of hope who inspire hope. What
a refreshing read!"

Cardinal Timothy M. Dolan
Archbishop of New York

"An astute examination of the enduring gift that Christ
gives in the priesthood and the spiritual challenges all
priests face in the modern world. From his years of pastoral care and scholarly research, Rossetti provides wise
and welcome advice to priests, young and old alike, for
living a fruitful priesthood and being energizing agents
for the New Evangelization. It is a pleasure to recommend this thoughtful and serene reflection on why we
should be so joyful in our priestly ministry."

Cardinal Donald Wuerl
Archbishop of Washington

"These letters will benefit any priest or bishop who reads
them. They are written by a happy and holy priest who
has spent many years working with brothers who have,
sadly, lost their way. This experience gives his meditations
a particular depth, pungency, and power. Msgr. Rossetti
knows that the priesthood is, for the vast majority of
priests, a path that leads to tremendous fulfillment, peace,
and joy. This collection of beautifully written essays
shows forth his love for the priesthood and for those
who strive to walk this challenging and wonderful path."

Rev. Robert Barron
Word on Fire Catholic Ministries

"Letters are the classical style in which friends communicate their deepest desires and sentiments to one another. For two thousand years in our Catholic tradition, we have used letters to both individuals and communities in order to encourage, inspire, and challenge. Msgr. Rossetti has done just that in this book. These letters of gratitude from a joyful priest remind us how blessed each of us is by the ministry of priests in our lives. For those of us who have been called to the priesthood, he reminds us of the privilege and awesome responsibility to faithfully live it out as servants and friends of Jesus Christ. Rossetti encourages each of us to allow the New Evangelization to be made manifest through our life and ministry."

Msgr. David L. Toups
Rector of St. Vincent de Paul Regional Seminary
Boynton Beach, Florida

"In the heart of the Year of Faith and the excitement surrounding the election of Pope Francis, Msgr. Rossetti offers a New Evangelization of sorts for priests. In a heartfelt collection of letters written to his brother priests, Rossetti gives witness to hope and new life within the context of priestly ministry as we move into the future as Church. With a spirit of profound humility, his letters are encouraging, poignant, and often challenging: filled with courageous zeal for the priesthood of Jesus Christ. Priests and seminarians alike will find wisdom, thoughtful reflection, and love to spur them on in their lives and ministries as they point others to encounter our risen Lord, Jesus Christ."

Msgr. Ross A. Shecterle
Rector of Sacred Heart School of Theology

LETTERS to My BROTHERS

Words of Hope and Challenge for Priests

Stephen J. Rossetti

Author of *Why Priests Are Happy*

ave maria press AMP notre dame, indiana

Nihil Obstat: Rev. Mark P. Kaminski, *Censor Librorum*

Imprimatur: Most Rev. Robert J. Cunningham
Bishop of Syracuse
Given at Syracuse, New York on 16 May 2013

Founded in 1865, Ave Maria Press is a ministry of the United States Province of Holy Cross.

www.avemariapress.com

Paperback: ISBN-10 1-59471-461-4, ISBN-13 978-1-59471-461-0

E-book: ISBN-10 1-59471-462-2, ISBN-13 978-1-59471-462-7

Cover image © Robert Harding Picture Library Ltd / Alamy.

Cover and text design by John Robert Carson.

Printed and bound in the United States of America.

Library of Congress Cataloging-in-Publication Data is available.

With gratitude to Chris Fabre, Bishop John McCormack, Msgr. Rob Panke, and Msgr. J. Wilfrid Parent for their kind assistance in reviewing the manuscript and their helpful comments.

Contents

Introduction

My brothers, these are difficult times. I do not need to tell you. No doubt, for the Church, every age has its joys and its challenges. But I sense a time, rapidly approaching, that will be particularly difficult. Washington's Cardinal Donald Wuerl recently spoke of a tsunami of secularism sweeping across our land. Have entire populations of people ever distanced themselves so far from God? For we who are "men of God," this can be especially trying and, at times, painful.

This is the reason for my letters. For a couple of years now, I have felt a growing desire to speak to you as one brother to another, from my heart to yours. I share with you my own reflections on our lives as priests today, as the tsunami washes over us. As one simple priest, these reflections are not the voice of authority, although I hope that the Spirit is somewhere in these letters, no matter how hidden. Nor are these letters the result of any external prodding. They are only the insights and inspirations arising from my heartfelt prayers for you. May they help prepare us both for the trials ahead.

Embodied in these letters is my vision of what is taking place these days on the surface and some of what might be hidden from first glance. It is the vision of a priest. I see much that is troublesome and, at times, alarming. But I see much more that consoles, encourages, and, at times, even elates. Ultimately, the work of God can never be thwarted. At root, there is in us a confidence and an optimism born of the Spirit. These can never be extinguished.

The majority of my priesthood has been spent with you—for over twenty years as a therapist, confidant, consultant, formator, and spiritual director for priests. When I stepped down from the leadership of a healing program for clergy, the Apostolic Nuncio publicly said, "Only God can reward you for your ministry." I responded as I truly felt: "He already has."

We have already been through a lot together. These have not been easy days. But through it all, I think we have gotten stronger. Perhaps it is because we have seen where secularism and sin lead. Before them is only the darkness. We must cry out. Perhaps a few hearts will turn and return. Conversely, we have witnessed where grace and holiness lead. This has filled our hearts with increasing joy. Tasting such truth, we are ever more strongly convicted in our priestly life and in our faith.

This must be the role of the priest today. You and I can see what is happening. It is becoming ever clearer and ever more apparent. The choice before the people is coming ever more sharply into focus. We, like the prophet Jeremiah, are impelled to speak out (see Jer 20:9). Like St. Paul, we say, "For an obligation has been imposed on me. Woe to me if I do not preach it!" (1 Cor 9:16).

In the midst of such darkness, the light inevitably shines more brightly. "But, where sin increased, grace overflowed all the more" (Rom 5:20). Perhaps this is why our time is so graced and so blessed. A few of our brothers would harken us back to some "golden age" of the priesthood and the Church, variously identified. But if there has ever been a golden age, it is now.

At times, these years have been harsh. And they are not over. We are still being purged. We are becoming more the priesthood we were meant to be. We are becoming holier. In the beginning, sanctity can taste bitter to the mouth, but the bitterness soon turns to sweetness in the soul.

It was not our intention to become holy men. We only heard the Lord's call and willingly chose to serve. But each year the bar has been raised a little higher. Each trial has caused us to dig a little deeper. Each ordeal has purified the priesthood a bit more. In the surrounding darkness, we begin to shine more brightly.

Where it began, prostrate on the floor, we would never have dreamt of such graces or prayed for them. We endure them now with faith. We welcome what is presented to us. We trust in the One who is worthy of trust. The best of presents comes from our God of divine gifts.

Today, I thank God for the divine gifts he has sent us. Today, I thank God for you.

Thank You, Father

My Brothers,

I begin these letters where I should begin, by thanking you. I am so grateful for you and your priesthood. From the very beginning until now, you have nurtured me in the faith, supported me as a brother, and shared with me the riches of God's beauty and truth. What a wonderful grace you have been for me. And so, I begin as I must by thanking you.

When I was just born, you welcomed me into God's family, pouring water over my head in the name of our triune God and casting out the powers of darkness. You anointed me with the oil of salvation. It was then that I became a member of God's redeemed family, thanks to you. For you, it was probably just another routine Sunday baptism, but not for me. For me, it was the beginning of everything.

I remember you teaching our catechism class. You taught us the faith. You shared with us your own faith. How could I believe if there was no one to share the

Word? You did that. I know you were very busy, but I could see that you enjoyed being with us. Your eyes twinkled a bit, I thought, and you had a big smile for us. I remember. I could tell the faith was precious to you, and so it became precious to me. I thank you.

You gave me my First Communion. By that time, I knew that there could be no Eucharist without a priest. You were there. There are parts of the world today without priests. They have no one to celebrate the Holy Eucharist. Today, even in this rich land, it is becoming poorer in the things of the Lord, including numbers of priests. You have remained faithful. You have remained steadfast in your priesthood, and so I have been blessed to receive the Lord's body and blood. Thank you, thank you, thank you. Whew! What would I have done without you?

You might not remember when I became an altar boy. Classes were on Sunday mornings in the parish hall. You were teaching the new servers the prayers at the foot of the altar in Latin, as they were in those days. I simply walked in unannounced and uninvited, and sat down. You didn't ask me why or what. You knew when to keep silent and to let things be. You simply and kindly accepted my presence and so I became one of them.

I liked being on the altar, although I don't think I understood too much, at least intellectually. I learned most from your gestures and your face. Your eyes were focused so intently during the consecration. Throughout, I heard the reverent tone of your voice and saw your actions. You taught me about the Eucharist.

I am not sure I was much of a help to you, really. You welcomed us. I felt welcomed by God. I felt at home there. You and I were surrounded by sacred things, things set apart for God's service. The symbols of cross and saint were part, and are part, of our beings. They and we are one community. It is where we belong. Thank you for sharing these with me.

In adulthood, each place I went, you were there—a faithful priest. Each Sunday you did your best when you preached. Some of you were better preachers than others. But each one spoke the truth. For ten or fifteen minutes each Sunday, we heard the truth preached to us. It was not a small thing. Today, many never hear the truth. All they hear is a cacophony of noise, superficial facts, and half-truths. Each Sunday, at Mass, we hear the truth and we receive the truth into our hearts.

At one point, you asked me if I ever considered becoming a priest. Was Jesus asking me through you? Through his Mother? Perhaps. But it was not yet a crystalized thought.

Clearly, I could see you and your example. You liked being a priest. I could see that people needed their priest and his presence was important to them. Indeed, what could be more important?

When a child was born or a parent died, when someone was to be married or someone was ill, they needed a priest and you were there. At times, it must have seemed mundane to you. But it was never so with us. When we were sick, it was not a small thing to have you enter our room.

These are important moments to us, and we want a priest to stand among us. We want God to be among us. I know that God is always here, but when the priest comes, it is a unique presence. You truly act *in persona Christi*. Many people love you, some people hate you; it is the same with Jesus. Thus, it will always be.

When I started to think about priesthood, it was you who came to mind. You showed me what priesthood was. This was important. I know you weren't perfect. I didn't expect you to be. But I expected you to be faithful, and you were.

When I entered the seminary, it was you who taught me and formed me. God knows I wasn't the easiest of seminarians. I was anxious to get going, I didn't want to spend so many years studying. You were patient. You taught me scripture, systematics, sacraments, moral theology, and preaching. You supervised my pastoral work, and I learned from you how to be a priest. I made some mistakes. But you were patient.

Do you remember when I was in the seminary and they were thinking of dismissing me? God knows I was a bit hardheaded and stubborn. But you went and literally pounded on their desks (so uncharacteristic for such a gentle man!). Reluctantly, they kept me on. Thank you, Father. I needed someone in my corner precisely at that moment. It was, of course, a priest who intervened. Did God send you?

And so I was ordained. On my ordination day, you were there. After the bishop, you laid your hands on my head. Those actions said it all. We partake of the one loaf, the one cup, the one Spirit. We are brothers united in the Lord.

Now, after many years, I am happily ensconced in priesthood. I continue to be blessed surrounded

by priests. You are my brothers. We pray together,
go to the movies and out to dinner, and we travel
on vacations together. I am grateful to be part of a
priest-support group, Jesu Caritas. We have been meeting monthly for over a dozen years. You know me well,
and we support each other.

You continue to hear my confession, and you hold
me up when things get rough. There have been some
difficult times these last years. We have not always been
the Church that we have been called to be. But the
public lashing, at times, has been incredible. The fury
of hell has been unleashed against us.

Perhaps worse are the judgmental criticisms, snide
comments, rageful bloggings, and general dismissal.
Some see us as anachronisms or figures from a past,
superstitious era. Others simply do not care. I feel sad
that they do not receive joy or take in Love's bountiful
self-gift. Their ragings and anger, if not checked, will
lead to death.

During it all, you have been oh-so-steady. Mass
after Mass. Baptism after Baptism. Sick call after sick
call. Kindness after kindness. I marvel at you and wonder what it is that sustains you. The cup I drink of, you
shall drink. Every era has its crucifixions and its exalta-
tions. We have ours. I have heard it said that the angels
only envy us in that they cannot suffer for God as we
can. In these days, the angels must be very envious.

Whenever my faith is weak, I only need look at
your face to be strengthened. Together we are strong.
Together we are priests. It is our faith, not my faith. It
is our priesthood, not my priesthood. I would not be

a priest were it not for you, and I would not be able
to remain a priest were it not for you.

Together we have been supported by the people.
They, too, are our friends and our family. Their love
for us feels so much more than we have any right to
deserve. It is really their love for Jesus. I hope they see
a little of him in us. I trust that they do. That can be
the only explanation for such a generous outpouring
of love for such flawed souls as ours.

It has been many years since I was ordained. Slowly,
I saw you, Father, get old and finally pass away. You
ministered until the end. I don't think I have the
strength or the great generosity to be the priest that
you were. You were a generation of holy men. You
formed us and you nurtured us. I would not be a priest
today without you.

Now, finally, I belong to the older generation of
priests. There are younger priests now. I rely on them,
their enthusiasm and their energy. I love their zeal,
although at times it needs a little softening. They could
use a little more patience. But that will come. Perhaps
I can help with that.

And they can help me. I need them. I move a little
slower. I need their energy. I tire more easily. They
kindly raise my drooping hands. I need their faith. We
are priests together.

I thank you, Father, for what you have done for me.
I thank you, my brothers, for our common priesthood
and our common faith. It is because of you I am here
today. It is because of you that priests will be here
tomorrow.

A crowd seated around him told him, "Your mother and your brothers [and your sisters] are outside asking for you." But he said to them in reply, "Who are my mother and [my] brothers?" And looking around at those seated in the circle he said, "Here are my mother and my brothers. [For] whoever does the will of God is my brother and sister and mother."

—Mark 3:32–35

Sharing Our Joy

My Brothers,

Did you see the movie *The Golden Compass?* Very entertaining I thought. However, the movie portrayed a dark and sinister authority over the people called the "Magisterium" that stunted their freedom. The "Magisterium" perpetrated "dogmas" that were repressive and strangled people's humanity and desire for the truth. It was not hard to perceive this thinly veiled criticism of Christianity and, especially, Catholicism.

The movie reflected a widespread public perception today that religion is a repressive, man-made reality that stifles human happiness and freedom. According to this view, if people want to be truly free, happy, and fully human, they need to throw off the repressive yoke of religion and become secular humanists. Thus, it is fashionable to say today, "I am spiritual but not religious." People profess to have some spirituality, but they do not want to be "restricted" by a religion. Indeed, who would want to belong to a repressive religion that perpetrates constricting man-made dogmas? Not I, for sure.

Repeat a lie often enough and people start to believe it. The secular lie has been repeated often. One of our challenges is that we priests are "in the world, but not of the world." Since we are in the world, we hear many truths, some half-truths and some lies as well. Many of us are almost starting to believe, at least on a subconscious level, the secular lie that religion makes you unhappy and unfree.

I remember an incident, in the sacristy of a church a few years ago, when I was speaking with the pastor just before Mass was about to begin. He is a fine priest and one of our best shepherds. He had read some of my research on priestly happiness and took exception to it. He said adamantly, "Priests are not happy." He became quite animated about it and rather upset that my data indicated that about 90 percent of priests report being happy. Finally, just as we were about to process out for Mass, I asked him, "Well, Father, how about you? Are you happy as a priest?" "Oh, yes," he replied strongly, "I like being a priest. But the others are unhappy."

Many of us are starting to believe that priests are unhappy. The lie has been repeated often in the press, and a few unhappy priestly souls especially have propagated it. And why shouldn't it be true? The child abuse crisis, the lack of priests, the thrashing we have taken in the press, the "onerous burden" of celibacy, and the "poverty" of our lives must all be conspiring to dishearten us. Certainly secular society today could only conclude that priests must be unhappy. How could priests possibly be happy under such terrible circumstances? But when researchers actually ask priests, again and again, the survey results are consistent—about 90 percent of priests say they are happy.

This does not mean it is unanimous. There are indeed about 10 percent of priests who are not happy. I reported this data in a gathering of about 150 priests and their bishops. One priest adamantly protested and was vociferous in his objection. Finally, a bit exasperated, I said, "I didn't say everyone was happy. You could be one of the 10 percent." Later the chancellor took me aside and said, "He is one of the 10 percent."

Numerous surveys of priests in the United States conducted by various organizations using different samples and different techniques have all come up with the same results: about 90 percent of priests report being happy as priests. This number is, incidentally, much higher than the general population. Not only are the vast majority of priests happy, but also they report much higher happiness levels than the general population.

Of course, this does not mean that you and I like everything about priesthood today. One need only sit down with a group of priests to hear a litany of all the problems. You know them as well as do I. But clearly these problems do not keep priests from, at their core, finding happiness and satisfaction in our vocation and priestly ministry. At root, it is a meaningful and satisfying life.

The great lie of secularism has been spoken so often that people are starting to believe it. More than a few are casting off the "repressive yoke" of religion and Catholicism. As rates of religious practice decrease, what has been the result? Are people happier today? In fact, it is no wonder that happiness rates among Americans are not rising, and some researchers have suggested they have actually been declining over the last few decades.[1] While it is likely that there are many causes, people who belong to an active faith community are consistently shown to be happier than those outside of religious practice.

Did you see Al Pacino's masterful character portrayal in *The Devil's Advocate*? He plays the role of Satan, disguised as a lawyer. He gives a marvelous soliloquy in which Satan puts forth his vision for man. He complains against God, saying that God gives people an "extraordinary gift" of their humanity but tells them not to use it: "Look but don't touch. Touch but don't taste." Satan concludes, "He's a sadist." On the other hand, Satan says, "I'm a fan of man. I'm a humanist." These are the half-truths that have twisted the mind of modern humanity: God and religion frustrate human desires; secularism leads to freedom, self-fulfillment, and happiness. It is little wonder that Jesus called Satan the "father of lies."

Secularism says it promotes "science," but true science has consistently demonstrated that religion is actually good for you and a necessary part of a healthy human life. It makes you happier and healthier; religious people actually live longer. That's just in this life. In the next, it might just help you get into heaven! The social sciences have demonstrated that priestly service brings the highest levels of satisfaction of any vocation or job in the country.[2] When science is accomplished with integrity, it cannot help but point to the truth.

Such truth is hard for the secular mind to accept. Some become irritated when they hear it and insist there must be some mistake. On the other hand, where does atheistic secularism truly lead? It leads to unhappiness and unfreedom. It is a dead end. Our society is slowly discovering this truth. Some are beginning to react against the "freedom" that began in the 1960s and 1970s. Not finding the deep happiness that it promised, they are looking again to our churches and to God.

We will offer them the same faith that we have always professed. Jesus Christ is the same yesterday, today, and forever. But this faith must be encoded in the language and culture of today. The New Evangelization is our faith enfleshed in the twenty-first century. If at times people have not responded to the faith, we priests must share part of the blame for not always presenting the joyful, merciful face of Christ in the language of today.

We must speak of the joy and happiness that people so desperately seek. We offer them the freedom that only Jesus can bring. God is love and God is joy. The offer of Isaiah stands: "All you who are thirsty, come to the water! You who have no money, come, buy grain and eat; Come, buy grain without money, wine and milk without cost" (Is 55:1).

Most importantly, they need to see the joy that is in our lives as priests and in our communities of faith. It is there. It is time to share it with the world.

Father, are you happy as a priest? If the clock were turned back, would you prostrate yourself again and be ordained? The vast majority of priests, 90 percent, say yes, even in these difficult times. I suspect you would as well.

It is good to step back from time to time and look at the big picture. You and I can get frustrated about many things—all the mail from the chancery, the incessant requests, the unreasonable demands, the never-ending stream of phone calls, insistent knocks on the door, and the bottomless pit of human needs.

I do not mean to minimize the challenges. I know you get frustrated and that the demands on you are unreasonable. I wish you had another priest or two in your rectory to help you. I wish you didn't have to open the newspaper and every other day read some scandalous story about priestly misconduct. I wish you had time to rest a little each day, eat a meal in peace, and take a proper vacation.

But let us step back a moment and look at the big picture. When we priests take such moments, we see that we are needed and loved. People are grateful for their priests. Looking at the many Christmas cards and the little gifts we receive, the many words of thanks and grateful smiles, we know that our lives are intensely meaningful to people. Priesthood is about ultimate meaning.

We priests realize that we are truly blessed. We are blessed to minister to and with such terrific people of faith. We are blessed to belong to a fraternity of brothers in the priesthood. We are infinitely blessed to be loved by such a God as ours.

We do not envy those who do not darken the doors of our Church. Private spirituality without a community of faith cannot flourish as it should. It is in the Church, the gathered people of God, that Christ is most powerfully and fully present. Through the Church that Jesus founded, God showers the fullness of his divine life and joy upon us.

You and I have been given great gifts—the gift of our faith and the gift of the priesthood. Priesthood is first and foremost a gift for others. We are priests for the people. They deserve our best, our devoted service—this service you so generously give. But priesthood is also a gift for us. Our self-giving is returned as a gift to us. As we pour out ourselves in service, we become more and more like Christ, who is the incarnation of God's love and joy.

As we give of ourselves to others, the blessing returns to us one hundredfold. Why do priests report such a strong degree of happiness despite such challenging conditions? How could we not be happy when surrounded by such faith-filled people and suffused with the Spirit of our loving God! I often remember the words of an old priest upon his retirement. The Vicar for Clergy asked him about his fifty-plus years of priestly service. The old priest, with a kindly face, looked up, wistfully smiled, and said, "It was a wonderful blessing. I wish I could do it all over again."

A Descent into Hell

Dear Brothers,

I awoke this morning and, as usual, I spent time with the Lord. Then, as my thoughts often do, they turned to you, my brothers. I think of you, and I am glad. You have little in the way of this world's riches. Public support for you and religion continues to decline. Yet each morning you too rise and rededicate yourself to serving God and the people. Despite it all, your happiness and satisfaction levels are very high. In fact, the numbers suggest that they are actually rising. Should people need any other sign to believe? Your joy is the best sign.

Your joy attracts people to the faith and to a priestly vocation. I remember when I was in Taiwan serving in the military. I got to know the Maryknoll fathers and sisters well. Many of them served as missionaries on this small island for their entire lives. What struck me was their happiness and enthusiasm. They had very little in the way of material possessions. They were practically ecstatic when I bought them a little motorbike. Yet they were always grateful people. Shortly after this experience, I began to consider a vocation.

In contrast, a few years ago I "descended into hell." I was in London for a meeting and had a free evening. I always enjoy going to the West End, hoping to catch one of those fantastic British theater productions. I arrived a little early and noticed a line forming outside one of the theaters. So I walked over and said to the young man, "Why are you standing in line?" He answered with a smile and a nice British clip, "We're Brits—we always queue up!" So I decided to queue up behind him, still not knowing what was about to occur.

Then a man raised a ticket over his head and said, "I have an extra ticket, five pounds." "I'll take it," I quickly shouted. Whatever this event was, it was sold out and people were clamoring for tickets. I bought the ticket and still had no indication of what the event was. There was no sign on the theater either. I walked inside the fairly large theater and sat down amidst a packed crowd. After a short while, a man, whom I had never heard of, walked out on stage: Christopher Hitchens. He was promoting his new book, *God Is Not Great: How Religion Poisons Everything*. It turns out, he was a famous atheist.

For over an hour, Hitchens ranted and espoused his atheistic doctrine to the cheers of the crowd. He explicitly rejected God, all religion, and the next life. At one point he shouted, "Christianity is evil rubbish!" Everyone loudly cheered. I thought he looked awful. His face was reddened and his complexion pallid. Throughout the night, he was enraged and spouted his hatred for all things divine. The crowd was wild with enthusiasm. I thought I had descended into hell.

Some time later, Christopher Hitchens was diagnosed with esophageal cancer. He remained a committed atheist and hostile to religion throughout his illness. During an interview he said it would be a "kindness" to visit dying Catholics and say to them, "Hope you don't mind, you said you were Catholic? Only three weeks to live? Well, listen, you don't have to live them as a mental slave, you know; you could have three weeks of freedom from fear of a priest. Don't be a mug all your life."[3]

Sadly, a few months ago, he died. I pray for him. Perhaps this is one of the reasons the Spirit led me to the theater that evening. I do believe I was meant to be there. It was an important moment for me to hear what such people think and believe today. It was madness and yet they could not see it. The room was whipped into a kind of satanic frenzy. I can only describe it as a taste of hell.

God knows you and I have probably scared off a few people ourselves. Sadly, some do suffer from "fear of a priest." None of us priests have always been the kind, loving shepherds of souls we should be. And I feel as though I am getting a little more "gruff" as I get older. I think I am starting to become a bit more like the stereotype of the older, slightly gruff (but hopefully lovable!) monsignor.

Yes, you and I must take some of the blame for those who leave. If our Church was more loving, more welcoming, more pastorally compassionate, and more joyful, we would certainly have more parishioners. A

few people have told me that the Church has a repu-
tation for being stiff, authoritarian, and somber, with
mediocre homilies and lifeless services. The stereotype
is exaggerated to be sure, but there is some truth to it.

While we can and must try to do better, I personally believe the modern sliding away from the Church
is not primarily the result of the weaknesses and failings
of our Church, although many believe it so. In truth,
the Church has always been imperfect at best and, at
times, downright scandalous. I thoroughly appreciated reading a historical account of the "bad popes."
This is probably a good book to read right now. It
reminds us how bad things were, right at the apex of
our Church's leadership, a few hundred years ago. It
makes us appreciate the sanctity of our recent popes
and how fortunate we are to have the priests and bishops of today. We are fortunate.

Instead, I believe that the modern exodus from religion has more to do with the changes in modern society and the draining away of faith than it does with any
limitations of our Church and its clergy. The Church
has always been led and staffed by imperfect people.
Rather, there is something new happening. There is
something new in the wind that is desiccating people's
faith. I think you can sense it.

The winds of a new human self-sufficiency are
blowing. There is a new age of "reason" emerging,
and people are caught up in their own abilities to
experiment, to invent, to feed, and to cure. Such scientific and technological advances are to be lauded and
used to the betterment of humankind. But, sadly, the
human consciousness is now increasingly eclipsing the

divine horizon beyond it. One day, people will recognize the limits of the human and ask again if there is One who is not limited. But for now, they are caught up in their self-sufficiency.

I once attended a friend's dinner party on a wealthy island. He was a practicing Catholic and a fine man. At one point in the evening his well-heeled and highly educated guests asked me about my being a priest and about Catholicism. Not letting such an opportunity go by, I launched into a simple exposition of the kerygma and the Good News of Jesus. The people listening barely reacted; it was as if I was speaking of a completely alien world.

After the party was over my host said, "Father, it's not that they are bad people, but they have never heard of these things before." If Hitchens represents a smaller group of explicit, militant atheists, there are many, many more who are functional atheists. They are not so much against the idea of God and religion. Rather, God and religion have no apparent meaning or relevance in their lives.

Among such functional atheists, faith is not nurtured because it is not seen as necessary. They have everything they need at their disposal, or so they think. But there are moments when this bubble of self-sufficiency bursts, at least for a limited time: the diagnosis of a serious disease, the death of a loved one, the dissolution of a family, acts of terror, war, and violence . . . these moments often shatter the illusion of human self-sufficiency, if only for a moment. Then people may look to us for answers. Then they may ask questions that they have never asked before.

In the end, it is a question of faith. Faith is the ultimate and real choice of life. Will they come to believe
in a God who made them out of love and has a plan for
each of them? Will they accept the offer of forgiveness
in Jesus? Will they let themselves be loved by God? In
the end, they will choose to serve in thanksgiving or
they will refuse to bow their heads. This is the perennial human choice and the perennial challenge of faith.
Despite our technology and our scientific advances, the
core challenge fundamentally remains the same.

The human soul has an innate desire for the truth.
It wants to believe; it was made to believe. The militant
atheist tortures his mind and his soul. I glimpsed this
torture and its heavy price that night with Christopher
Hitchens. Today's larger group, the functional atheists,
leave the space made for God in their hearts unfilled.
Can the rest of the organism really live without him?
I wonder if the final result for both is the same—the
death of all that is truly human.

Our hearts and souls were made for God. We
innately sense his existence. What is most unreasonable
and does the greatest violence to the human intellect
is atheism. Today's arrogance of mind threatens to
overshadow our innate sense of God. Our corrupted
reason blinds our hearts.

My brothers, let us begin this day anew, thanking God. We see so many good people in this world
who apparently have no explicit faith. It becomes so
very apparent that the faith we have is God's gift to
us and thus gratefully received. In the time of Jesus, a
few were invited to leave their homes and follow him.
Today, we are the ones whom he has invited.

Thank you Lord. Thank you for having invited us to follow you. Thank you for the gift of faith. The eyes of faith that are your gift to us allow us to see you, to know you, and to love you. May we be your instruments so that others might know you and love you. Together, may our lives be a song of thanksgiving and a perpetual act of love.

A Voice That Will Never Be Silenced

My Brothers,

The forces conspiring against the Church and the faith seem to be growing. Can you sense the change? On the surface, we recognize that the fastest-growing "religious denomination" in the United States today is "unaffiliated." Most of these people have dropped out of mainstream Christian communities, including the Catholic Church. Some of you have parishes bulging at the seams with parishioners; others do not. I suspect many of you can sense a slow and growing change. Things are not the way they were when you were a child.

Many of the newly unchurched would say, "I am spiritual but not religious." They do not attend any church, nor do they practice in a faith community. They will likely not teach their children about the faith or give them a religious upbringing. When their children grow up, religion will be entirely foreign—something neither considered nor experienced. Their children's mantra will likely be, "I am neither spiritual nor religious." We see signs of this already. Secularism is spreading.

I recently read a serious essay in a prominent journal in which the author was lamenting the death of her beloved mother. This obviously intelligent woman was struggling with where her mother had gone in death. Both her parents were fallen-away Catholics, and as their daughter she clearly had no religious upbringing. Thus, she could not answer the question of where her mother had gone. After a lengthy, tortured reflection, she ended up concluding that her mother was now in the trees, in the clouds, and all around her—a pantheistic, impersonal presence in nature. It was a pretty sad conclusion.

With the waning of faith, we should not be surprised that assaults on our religious values and our Church are increasing. The freedom to practice our faith appears to be eroding. The US government has been trying to force Catholic organizations to fund contraceptive practices. Religious freedom was one of the prime motivators for our ancestors coming to this new land. Through the judicial system and in the public forum, we are fighting for these freedoms again.

Marriage is being redefined. The word "Christmas" is being struck from people's mouths. There are fewer mentions of God in the public forum for fear of offending. Public prayer is often restricted if not outright prohibited (except ironically in Congress where a prayer is recited each day!).

The respect for human life is in danger. Abortions and a contraceptive mentality keep many more from coming into this world. Populations in the more prosperous nations will dwindle significantly. There are even serious attempts at passing laws legalizing euthanasia. As Cardinal Seán O'Malley said in the 2013 national Pro-Life Mass, "A society that allows parents to kill their children will allow children to kill their parents."[4] The gulf between Christianity and the world is increasing. Our life and our values are increasingly countercultural.

This is on the outside. This is what you can see. These changes are a clear eroding of our Christian heritage and a seeping secularism. But hidden underneath is something more fundamental, more primitive. You can sense it just under the veneer of "civilized" actions. It seems to me that there is a growing anger toward the Church. When you scratch below the surface, the disdain and anger become more apparent. Have you seen it?

If you take off the veneer, there is a growing denigration of the Church and God's revelation that it preaches. For some, there is a desire to discredit, as if to justify their own secularism. For others, there is even a desire to destroy. God knows we are not perfect, but from whence comes this hostility against Church? From whence comes the seething anger for all things of God?

The scriptures suggest that there is ultimately one place. It is a battle that began before time. Ever since Satan, God's most powerful angel, turned his back, he has been ever set on destroying the Church and the faith. "He will strike at your heel" (Gn 3:15). But he has miscalculated . . . badly. For "the gates of hell shall not prevail against it" (Mt 16:18). Is this battle raging in our world today?

Because of our failings, at times despicable, we have rightly deserved some of this public lashing. We cannot complain when we are justly accused of our sins and misdeeds. But the hatred with which the lash is wielded by a few and the intensity of the beating some inflict suggest that there are "unresolved issues," as we psychologists like to say.

Richard Dawkins, well-known atheist and author of *The God Delusion*, was one of the leaders of the 2012 "Reason Rally" in Washington, DC. He publicly advocated that some religious beliefs, such as Catholic beliefs in the Eucharist, ought to be publicly "ridiculed with contempt." He said, "Mock them! Ridicule them! In public!"[5] Would that have been said on the National Mall in our nation's capitol fifty years ago? I suggest that there is nothing more contrary to reason than atheism. Right use of reason leads us to the divine. While Dawkins's extremism represents only a minority, it is symptomatic of a trend that we cannot afford to ignore. Something has changed.

This new climate is particularly difficult if we priests and bishops want to be liked and accepted by everyone. Indeed, who wants to be hated? Only a masochist. We priests are mostly people who want to be loved by all. We like to think of ourselves as "nice guys." Why would anyone want to hate us? Why indeed? The scriptures remind us of our lot: "They will hand you over to the courts and scourge you. . . . You will be hated by all because of my name, but whoever endures to the end will be saved" (Mt 10:17, 22).

The scriptures also tell us that we are engaged in a battle that began before time and will continue until the end. Do we believe it? Satan and his minions, including all those on this earth who do their father's will (Jn 8:44), are bent on destroying the faith and the Church. We see this most dramatically during an exorcism. The demons practically spit when they say the word "priest"; their disdain is palpable. A few of us have been spit at in recent days. It may be that we are seeing concrete examples of this spiritual conflict in our world today.

I must admit I find it unnerving when people focus their attention on me with so much rage. It is upsetting to feel their hostility and their anger. These past few years I have been surprised at the hostility directed at priests in a variety of settings, whether in casual social gatherings, in public, or in print. And this anger is not only among those who profess atheism; at times, there are moments of unconverted hostility even among those who believe.

Many do not believe in the existence of hell or Satan anymore. Or, perhaps conceding the possibility of hell, they posit that it is empty. After experiencing a bit of this life, I am convinced in the existence of both. Just as there are many wonderful signs and foretastes of heaven, sadly, there are more than a few signs of hell's cruelty and depravity.

There is only one source of peace. "Peace I leave with you, peace I give to you" (Jn 14:27). If we do not accept the peace of Christ, there is only one alternative. It will begin with mild frustration. It will grow into disdain and arrogance. It will lead to anger and "righteous" indignation. Ultimately, it must end in a consuming rage. When one rejects heaven, one is left with the only alternative—hell. No one can abstain from choosing. The ultimate choice, quite simply, is peace or rage.

This is why we must redouble our efforts. More than a few souls are increasingly angry and, from there, it is only a short step into the darkness of rage. We offer them Jesus, the peace of souls. The task might seem increasingly overwhelming, as the cloud of secularism spreads a deepening gloom. But God's grace pierces through, again and again.

You and I are privileged, time and again, to witness miracles of grace. They confirm our faith and our priesthood. We anoint a dying woman and see the radiance of heavenly joy in her face. We witness young people turning to Jesus during World Youth Day, with some entering the seminary. We experience souls weeping in the confessional. We are buoyed by the beaming face of a newly received member during the Easter Vigil. There are many graced moments in our priesthood.

In this era of iPhones, iPads, Wi-Fi, and social networking, fundamental human desires are unchanged. Our message and the divine gifts that Jesus offers through us are no less relevant today than they were in the beginning. When the day is done and people open their hands, what will be in them? Joy or despair? Peace or rage? Light or darkness? This is the fundamental choice. No one is exempt.

You offer them joy; you offer them peace; you speak of the only light that can dispel their darkness.

You speak of our divine destiny. Your voice, because it is his voice, will never be silenced.

Some of the Pharisees in the crowd said to him, "Teacher rebuke your disciples." He said in reply, "I tell you, if they keep silent, the stones will cry out!"

—Luke 19:40

Underestimating Sin

Dear Brothers,

You might know that I ministered to priests for seventeen years in a residential treatment center. It was a unique privilege for which I give heartfelt thanks. The priests came to us with a variety of psychological issues. Mixed in with these weaknesses of the psyche were typically a combination of bad choices, human failings, and sinful actions. In addition to suffering psychological ailments, some were suffering the effects of their own mistakes and sins.

I would be remiss, my brothers, if I did not say a word about it: sin—an ugly topic to be sure, but too important to ignore. It pains me to see the personal destruction that it causes. In these modern times, we have rightly emphasized the loving mercy of God. More people are drawn to a "spoonful of honey" than a "barrelful of vinegar," according to St. Frances de Sales. It is true. But, in the process, we seem to have underestimated and overlooked the deadly reality of sin.

We do our people and ourselves a disservice when we do not speak the truth about sin at all. I must speak about it with you. People do not like the word. You and I are both loath to mention it. Our confessionals are not as full as they used to be or should be. One man recently said to me, "Why should I go to confession? What do I do wrong? I am a good person." But the scriptures remind us, "If we say, 'We are without sin,' we deceive ourselves, and the truth is not in us" (1 Jn 1:8).

Distorted worldly attitudes about sin easily creep into our lives—attitudes that can make us too glib about sin. We priests are not immune from such distortion. Occasionally, priests dealing with habitual grave sin have told me, "Yes, it was a sin, but I confessed it and now it's gone." This is true. A confessed sin is gone in God's eyes. We are washed clean. But this statement was said in a kind of cavalier manner, as if it were a trifle. And, unfortunately, something does remain.

While the sin is forgiven, what remains are the effects of sin and of one's bad choices. The priest who has indulged his concupiscence for a dozen years typically does not walk out of the confessional with his proclivities erased and his increasingly disordered soul completely righted. Yes, Jesus saves us and forgives us all our sins. But there is a purification process needed before we can behold the fullness of the divine light. We either go through the needed purification in this life or in the next (i.e., purgatory). Catholics do not believe in "cheap grace."

I have heard it said, perhaps with tongue in cheek, that the ideal life is to engage in every possible worldly vice and then, at the last moment, "convert" on one's deathbed. Timing is everything with this strategy! But such a deathbed "conversion" would only be the final seal on a lifetime of selfish choices. It would not be a true conversion.

The longer one lives a life of sin and selfishness, the farther and farther one travels from the light. While it is possible such darkened souls could convert, even on their deathbeds, it becomes increasingly unlikely. Souls that have increasingly plunged themselves into evil become increasingly inured to evil. They would no more want to taste the good things of God than saints would want to immerse themselves in evil. The choices we make slowly change us into beings full of light or full of darkness. The road back to the fullness of light can be a long one.

When priests walked through the door of our treatment program after years of substance abuse or sexual addiction, we knew theirs would be a long program of healing. Their intensive phase of residential treatment would be longer than most, and the aftercare process would last for years. They needed a long psychological and spiritual purgation. They needed to learn to develop and to love the virtuous pleasures of life such as real friends and the love of family. They also needed to learn to eschew the cheap highs of drugs and the dysfunctional thrill of illicit sex. They needed to learn to love the things of God and to abhor the taste of evil.

Initially, when one turns from evil, goodness still doesn't "taste" very good. It is a painful and difficult transition and transformation. The sex addict who has tasted illicit sex for many years often has problems initially appreciating licit love and sexual intimacy with his wife. The alcoholic in the midst of detox would hardly appreciate the satisfaction of a good meal; all he craves is the poison of alcohol. As St. Paul said, "I fed you milk, not solid food, because you were unable to take it" (1 Cor 3:2). It can require years of loving and tasting the good before we become accustomed to it and appreciate eating the real meat of God. It takes time before we fully recognize and abhor the fetid taste of evil.

When priests dealing with habitual grave sins have said to me, "Well, if I sin, I can just confess it and it is over," they have misunderstood the true nature of sin and forgiveness, and likewise missed the devastation left behind. Their theology is one of "cheap grace." Not too long ago, a bishop phoned me and was clearly exasperated. He said he had a priest in his diocese in his early seventies who had been discovered to have been living a double life of sexual licentiousness for many years. When the bishop confronted him, he admitted it but added, "What's the problem? I am good to the people." He did not understand why his bishop was so upset.

Priesthood, first and foremost, is not something that we do but something that we are. That priest's merely functional notion of priesthood and his misunderstanding of sin are striking. Is that all priesthood means, "Being good to the people"? Certainly that is important, but priesthood means so much more. And can a priest mired in horrific sin truly be a source of goodness for his people?

We ought to run from sin and be aghast at the mere thought of it. No good comes of sin. It is not a "little" thing, and its myriad effects are not so easily expunged.

Another deception clouding the modern mind today is, "Sin is fun." People believe that leading a life of virtue is unpleasant at best and usually downright disagreeable. The pleasures of sin seem enticing and are offered as a source of happiness. This is a deception. It is a lie. Although sin can briefly excite one's sensual pleasures, one need not wait long to discover how unhappy and tortured the sinner becomes. The sinner does not need to wait for hell in the next life to discover this. It is said, "Virtue is its own reward." I would add, "Sin is its own punishment."

Yes, evil has blinded our world to the darkness that sin causes. It is never fun, even in this life. Do you think drug addicts, alcoholics, sexual addicts, and child molesters "enjoy" their lives? Do you think they are living in a world of real love and peace? I have treated many of them, and every one was miserable. Do you think that the young people who engage in promiscuous premarital sex, contraception, and abortions are happier than their chaste counterparts of old? The path of modern psychic destruction is wide. Sin's only effect is misery and destruction.

My brothers, despite this sometimes austere life of self-giving and service that is ours, there is a strong current of true happiness among priests, as we have found. We are dedicated to the One who is good. We pour out ourselves in the loving service of others. We are immersed in the things of God, who is the only source of true human fulfillment and happiness. Thus, it is that we find ourselves increasingly filled with divine peace and a hint of his joy.

Priesthood is something more than what we do. You and I are priests. We have been uniquely configured to Christ and share most intimately in his life, including his loving relationship to the Father. It is from this intimate union with Jesus and our subsequent adoption in the Trinity that all of our lives flow. May no evil sully such a wonderful gift. The more we can be vessels and purveyors of such a great gift, the more the light will shine.

While the following scriptural citation applies to all Christians, it seems uniquely suited to you, my brothers.

You are the light of the world. A city set on a mountain cannot be hidden. Nor do they light a lamp and then put it under a bushel basket; it is set on a lampstand, where it gives light to all in the house. Just so, your light must shine before others, that they may see your good deeds and glorify your heavenly Father.

—Matthew 5:14–16

Faithful in Little Things

My Brothers,

I have been working with a few priests who "fell off the wagon." It was almost impossible to discern how the relapse initially began. It appeared to be a small, seemingly irrelevant decision. The recovering alcoholic who decides to "stop by" a store for a few items, a store that happens also to sell alcohol, may find himself plunging back into a relapse. Or the Internet sex addict who logs onto his computer to finish up a few parish items a bit too late at night, while he is tired and his defenses are down, may end up sliding into a full-scale relapse. What we learn is that no decision, however small, is ever irrelevant. Our choices always have consequences, for good or for ill.

For all of us, it is the daily, small decisions that when, combined together, set our course for each day and ultimately for our lives. This is precisely why the man who protested, "Why do I need to go to confession? I don't do anything wrong" was so mistaken. He was on the lookout for the big sins and the terrible crimes that would be clear markers of sin. Thus he missed the daily foibles and errors that eventually add up to big things. The saints all recognized their sinfulness. The person who professes to be "without sin" is likely on the wrong road.

As priests, we are aware of the "big" sins. For the celibate priest, genital sex is clearly out, regardless of the form it takes—with women, men, or children. Like our lay brothers and sisters, Internet pornography is on the prohibited list as well. Addictions of all kinds including alcohol and drugs are likewise not acceptable. We all know the list that will get you into a residential treatment program or potentially dismissed from ministry. Thank God the large majority of priests are free of such serious failings and sins.

But, as we strive to walk down the path to holiness, we ought to be mindful of the "lesser" clerical sins and failings. It is important that we become increasingly faithful in small things. I have found this as I get older; my personal bar of conduct is raised higher. As we live longer, I think we become more attuned and sensitized to what is good and what is evil, even in little things. And when we see "little" things in ourselves that are not quite right, we are increasingly less tolerant of them. They bother us more.

Getting drunk as a twenty-year-old is not good, but a sixty-year-old priest might also find it unseemly for him to drink to the point of being impaired or even tipsy. Foibles in one's twenties and thirties should be overcome as one ages with an ever-increasing faithfulness and attentiveness to the details. The bar gets raised as the years pass.

For each one of us, the details are different. Each one of us has our own "demons" that need to be exorcized from our lives. The man who is captivated by the senses will want to pay ever more detailed attention to the smaller sensual indulgences that are a trap for him. For the priest who struggles with material goods, he may need to drive a simpler car or stay away from expensive restaurants.

For the priest who is deficient in social relationships, he may actively pursue being kind to others. He may need to push himself to engage in meaningful pastoral encounters with people. Indeed, paying attention to the "little" things refers not only to avoiding the "little" sins but also engaging in the daily little acts of goodness that add up to a virtuous life.

There are some "little" failings that bear mentioning for all priests. My research has shown that priests who value the three promises they made at their diaconal and priesthood ordinations are more likely to be happier priests (and, I suspect, holier!).[6] These three promises are praying the Liturgy of the Hours, celibate chastity, and obedience. It is time to look at these again, more closely, and to rediscover their intrinsic value for our priestly lives today.

I remember a priest who came for residential care years ago. His priestly life had disintegrated. As is common in such circumstances, he had stopped praying some time ago. When I asked him about his promise to pray the Liturgy of the Hours, he said this was something for monks.

I have spent quite a bit of time with monks, and I can attest that chanting the Hours is indeed a central part of monastic life. However, the way the diocesan priest prays the Liturgy of the Hours is quite different but no less meaningful. For the priest in the world, praying the Hours means taking selected time throughout the day, in a daily rhythm of morning, midday, evening, and nighttime, and returning one's focus to the Beloved. The prayer of the Liturgy of the Hours is built around the scriptures, especially the Psalms. I find the Psalms often expressing my frustrations, hopes, and pleas in a poetic prayer. The "music" of the Psalms helps to give my inner self a voice, a sacred voice of the Word, when speaking to the Father.

The Liturgy of the Hours is especially important because it is a prayer of the Church, that is, it is a liturgical act in which we priests pray in the name of the Church for the people. Thus, not only is this prayer an important part of our personal day, it is also an important part of our ministry for the people. When we pray the Liturgy of the Hours, it is not a private prayer; it is the Church praying. It is for the people that we pray it.

In doing my research on priests' prayer practices, the data showed that those priests who did not pray the Liturgy of the Hours were much more likely to report not praying at all. Priests sometimes excused themselves from praying the Hours by saying that they will pray privately in another way. But the data show that this often does not occur. Over half of the priests in my survey (54 percent) who reported not saying the Hours reported praying a paltry fifteen minutes or less per day, while the average for the other priests was well over three times that amount. Priests who do not pray the Liturgy of the Hours are much more likely to be deficient in private prayer altogether. Unfortunately, only 56 percent of priests admit to praying "all or most" of the Hours daily. It is time to rethink this.

Another point, neuralgic for some as well, is our promise of obedience. Gathered around our bishops, we priests and people are the Church. The bishop is our shepherd, our leader, and the focal point of our unity. Our promise of obedience is easier when we like and trust our bishop. It becomes a real act of faith when we do not. And it is an even bigger act of faith when we realize that obedience to our bishop is part of a larger obedience to the universal Church. Our bishop represents the wider Church for us and is a direct link to it. When we promise to be obedient to our bishop and his successors, we not only promise obedience to a particular person, but we also promise to be obedient sons of the Church.

Embedded in our promise of obedience is an entire theology of the Church as founded and directed by Christ and the Spirit. Our promise of obedience is built on the belief, and thus to profess, that Jesus founded our Church and that this Church is unerringly moving, under the guidance of the Holy Spirit, to its final consummation in Christ. To promise obedience is to place oneself in the "stream" of this movement of grace or, said in another way, in the barque of Peter.

Staying in the barque includes big things, of course, like celebrating the Eucharist with reverence and faith, believing in sacred scripture as God's inspired Word, professing the creed with complete assent, and holding to the line of apostolic succession, including the primacy of Peter. It also ought to include the "little" things. Obviously, these are not as important from the standpoint of the hierarchy of beliefs, but they are important for our spiritual growth and pastoral integrity.

These "little" things might include more controversial items such as wearing clerical dress as stipulated for one's country or place of ministry; adhering to the rubrics of the Mass and sacraments; being careful with parish funds and taking only what is rightfully ours; and accepting a difficult assignment from the bishop with gratitude and without grumbling.

To set aside one's personal judgment and preference in deference to the universal Church is an act of faith and obedience. I do so, not because I agree with everything, but because I choose to do so, as an adult, as a priest, and as a man of faith. I trust in God that my obedience will bear fruit. I do not believe that every "little" decision from the hierarchy is a good one, but I do believe that God will bless my obedience and make it a source of grace.

I recall a young priest who left the ministry. He said, "I didn't leave the Church. The Church left me." He had a personal idea where the Church should go. He was not happy with the direction the Church actually went. Now where is he? He left the barque and is presumably on his own. This is not our understanding of the Church.

Our third promise is celibacy. There will be more on this in a later letter. But for now, it is a promise we made with full cognizance that it would be a lifetime commitment. Like a newly wedded couple, we could never know the full impact of our promises when we spoke them. But as it is for the married couple, it is an act of trust in God, which we renew and strengthen each day. We believe that it is he who is calling us to priesthood and to a celibate life. Whatever may come down the road, we trust in his faithfulness and generosity.

This promise of celibacy means more than simply not getting married or not engaging in sexual acts and sexual relationships (including Internet pornography!). It means being free to give ourselves completely to God and to the people in service. The celibate priest who spends an inordinate amount of time in his room on the Internet or excessively engaged in his own pleasurable pursuits is not truly celibate. He has taken on his own pleasures as a "spouse." Celibacy is not simply being single. The celibate priest is given to Christ and his Church. It is there that he finds his life and his calling.

Thus, a life of celibate integrity involves attention to the "little" things, including being available to the people, albeit in a reasoned, balanced way. Naturally, times of vacation and days off are important. But seasoned pastors know when to curtail one's vacation or to let go of a day off when, for example, a lifelong, faithful parishioner has died and ought to be buried by his or her pastor. Similarly, priests do not typically engage in ministry very late in the evening, but they are available when a member of the parish council is rushed to the emergency room in a life-threatening state.

Being celibate in "little" things also means not flirting or acting as if one was not committed. I regularly remind myself that I belong to God. While the celibate enjoys natural beauty, including the beauty of other human beings, appropriate celibate boundaries keep the celibate from engaging even in the very beginnings of a romantic process. The full and complete purification of our passions, so that we are faithful in "little" things, takes a lifetime of cooperating in God's grace.

The younger priests are not always alert to the dangers of the "little" things. They know about the "big" ones. Let us help them to be more vigilant, lest they unwittingly find themselves in an unwanted place. They may not know that, when it comes to sexuality, it is especially the "little" things that rapidly and progressively lead to greater. Younger men need your wisdom and guidance. Share it with them patiently and generously. And young priests should pay attention—you are listening to a man who has remained steady in the Lord's service, through years of adversity, temptation, and testing.

My brothers, you and I are on a journey to the living God. Because we love him, we want to give him our all. Priestly ministry in the world is no less of a journey for us toward sanctity and union with God than for the mystic or the hermit who breathes only the grace of God. As the years pass, we become faithful in the little things so that we are increasingly purified and prepared. We develop an increasing taste for all that is good and naturally develop a disgust of even the smallest amount of the fetid taste of evil.

We willingly choose all that is good, and we come to desire it fully with our hearts. My research found that the happiest of all the priests are the oldest ones. Are they happier because they no longer have the full burden of pastoral leadership and ministry? Perhaps. But we priests are also happier when we live more and more in the light. As even the smallest flecks of evil are expunged, our beautiful God can more fully fill us with his joyful presence. These older men have traversed the long purgation and are now purer vessels of the Spirit of God. All that we had hoped for and worked for is now just beginning.

His master said to him, "Well done, my good and faithful servant. Since you were faithful in small matters, I will give you great responsibilities. Come, share your master's joy."

—Matthew 25:23

Celibate Lovers

Dear Brothers,

I wanted to spend a moment with you speaking more fully about our commitment to celibate chastity, as I promised. I was watching a television show last night and a young woman, an Olympic athlete, spoke about her commitment to remain a virgin until marriage. She said it had been one of the hardest things she had ever done. She said she eventually wanted to give this gift to a future husband. What I found most fascinating was the response of the panel of middle-aged journalists and commentators. They were surprised, confounded, and incredulous. Everything else this Olympian said in the interview was lost. These educated people could only focus and marvel at such a commitment.

My, how things have changed! If the modern public can hardly believe a young woman would be able to be a virgin until marriage, how could it possibly understand or even believe someone could be celibate for life? This is the harsh environment that you and I enter as celibate priests.

Sexuality is a powerful gift from God in which we directly cooperate in divine creation. However, a powerful gift, when perverted, will necessarily become a powerful destructive force. By analogy, nuclear power is an incredible source of virtually unlimited energy; nuclear power is also the most destructive force known today. With it, we can power our world; with it, we can destroy our world. So, too, is sexuality for the psyche and spirit of man.

In today's climate, it seems to me that our priestly celibate commitment and witness are desperately needed. Expansive talk and incessant theologizing about celibacy can seem cheap and unconvincing to the modern mind. But the witness of a joyful celibate is a strong sign of the truth of the Gospel. If your priestly service was nothing more than a life of celibate integrity, it would be a much-needed homily.

Not an insignificant amount of human psychic destruction today comes from society's misuse of the creative power of sexuality. While you and I are compassionate with people who have sinned, we should never underestimate this point. Society has perverted the gift of sexuality, and it is paying a heavy price. People today will not listen to the Church regarding its various teachings on sexuality. But what might reach people's hearts is their experience of this destruction and conversely the liberating experience of true sexual integrity. When they experience the truth about human sexuality, it is a convincing teacher.

Like the prodigal son, society needs to wake up and see that its approach is not working. Like the prodigal son, people are wallowing in the mud and starving. I feel a great deal of compassion for them, as I know you do. They are not completely culpable. They have grown up with lies. They have grown up in an era when a group of educated adult commentators on a major national television network could be incredulous over a young woman who wanted to remain a virgin until marriage. Our society has lied to its children. Our children are suffering because of it.

"For the gate is wide and the road broad that leads to destruction, and those who enter through it are many" (Mt 7:13). When people realize that they are traveling the road to the destruction of their relationships, perhaps then they will be ready to try the way that Olympian suggested. In the meantime, we have a duty to warn people and a duty to teach the truth. Most importantly, and most efficaciously, we have an even more essential duty of living the truth and witnessing to it with our lives.

Conversely, whenever a priest falls into sexual sins, it weakens the Body of Christ. The media revels in it and people are scandalized. Admittedly, it is true that sins of the spirit are worse than sins of the flesh, but the power of human sexuality for good and for evil is great, including in our priests. We can "beget" life through the creative power of God working through us, or we can beget evil.

Nevertheless, chaste celibacy is much, much more than that for us. It is an important witness, to be sure. And, of course, it carries its own burdens. As we get older, the fires of human passion dwindle a little (just a little), but the desire for a mate in life does not. At each stage in life, the sacrifices of a celibate life are present. I do neither of us a service if I imply otherwise.

However, our pastoral experience shows us how difficult the vocation of marriage is as well. It is no less difficult than our vocation. We priests walk with many, many couples during the travails of their lives. You and I agonize with those whose marriages and families break apart. None of the couples that stood before us on the altar expected to get divorced. They all entered marriage with a heart full of happiness and the hope of a full life together. Even for those whose marriages remain intact, there are more than a few challenges and heartaches. Each vocation in life has its joys and its burdens.

Each vocation, married or celibate, needs to be lived with integrity and its riches mined and developed to be appreciated and to prosper. Married couples that do not work at their relationship and develop an intimate shared life of love and sacrifice will certainly not find the sacrament of marriage reaching its fullness in them. Similarly, you and I as priests will want to live our sacrament with integrity and a full self-giving. One of the major findings of my research on priesthood over the years is that those priests who live a priestly life as it is meant to be lived, and thus with integrity on all levels, are the happiest of priests. When we short-change our priestly lives, not only do the people suffer, we suffer too.

While there are many riches to be mined as celibate priests, two special joys ought to be mentioned. The first is our service and love for the people of God. The priest's relationship to them is unique. He is one of them and he is also set apart. He is a man for the people and a man of the people. No priesthood can be fully alive without a dynamic, loving connection to the people.

It is from the people that we receive so much love and support. I recall a saintly priest, now deceased, from my diocese. On his retirement from priestly ministry, his parish members held a wonderful celebration and poured out their love and affection for this great pastor. At the end of the Mass, he and I walked off the altar and I said, "Father Casey, how are these people going to live without you?" He looked me straight in the eyes and said, with a touch of sadness, "How am I going to live without them?" That simple comment said it all.

This is one of the reasons that priests must be men who can build healthy relationships. As Pope John Paul II said in *Pastores Dabo Vobis*, the priest is a "man of communion." An integral part of priesthood is building a community. We do so in the sacraments and most especially in the Eucharist. But this must also include building human relationships through our myriad encounters with the people.

The time we spend building relationships ought not to be undervalued. For example, standing outside the Church and greeting the people after a Sunday Mass seems like a small thing, but it is not. Imagine how people feel when they leave the Church and the pastor is nowhere to be found. It leaves a bit of an empty feeling in the congregation. Seeing their shepherd as they leave the Church, even if he was not the Mass's celebrant, is important to the people. He is a visible sign of their parish's communion.

There are many, many other ways that you build a community, whether it is visiting the homebound or the sick in the hospital, attending parish social functions, stopping into classes at the Catholic school, grieving with a bereaved family, or simply visiting a parishioner's home for a meal or cup of coffee. In these encounters, you help build a community of faith. In these encounters, we not only nourish the community but also find ourselves being supported and strengthened.

After years of being in a parish, we might be pleasantly surprised at how attached we have grown to these good people. Their faith, their goodness, and their love enrich our lives. As we pour out ourselves in service to them, the blessing is returned to us one hundredfold, as Jesus promised. One of the important riches of priesthood, especially for the celibate who has no family of his own, is our family of faith—the people who love and support us. Jesus said, "For whoever does the will of God is my brother and sister and mother" (Mk 3:35). As men configured to Christ, it is so for us as well.

Finally, and perhaps most importantly, the greatest of celibacy's riches is our relationship to our loving God. All people are called to be united to God in a loving communion. But Jesus, as the Son, had a unique relationship with his Father. It was this relationship that gave life and direction to Jesus' own being and ministry. One cannot understand who Jesus was and is without understanding his relationship to the Father.

While Jesus related to all of his disciples, he was especially close to twelve of them. They were his closest collaborators. They had a direct, daily, personal relationship to Jesus that was unique. We priests are uniquely configured to Christ. Thus, we too share directly in the life of Jesus. As celibates, a space is created in us for a relationship to the Father to grow in a particularly direct and conscious way. It is our great gift and our great necessity. It would be incomprehensible to us, and to the people, if a priest were not to nurture this relationship consciously, directly, and daily. We are men of God; we are lovers of God.

For too long the importance of a priest's direct relationship to God has been downplayed in those who are diocesan priests or in full-time ministry. We have tended to relegate praying to the monks and conversely to assign the work of ministry to active priests—ourselves. But prayer was an essential part of Jesus' life; apparently, he spent considerable time in communion with his Father. The active priest likewise finds his strength, direction, and peace in this indwelling God.

More will be said on prayer later, but I have been a bit surprised at my research's consistent findings of the importance of a priest's relationship to God for his personal happiness and contentment.[7] I would never have thought that a statistical research study could so strongly and clearly show the centrality for a priest of his relationship to God. But when you step back and think about it, it makes sense. How else could a celibate priest, who has dedicated his life to serving the

Lord, possibly find happiness or fulfillment without a strong connection with the God whom he serves?

God is never outdone in generosity. We have made this sacrifice for God. On his part, God stands waiting for us, ready to embrace us, even now. I have been to scores of convocations for priests on a wide variety of subjects. It is somewhat ironic that I do not remember even one dedicated to the priest's personal, loving relationship to God. This relationship is the pivot of a priest's life, and it is the gold of his celibate commitment.

When we make space for God, we are not disappointed with the divine generosity. The Father reveals everything to the Son and shares everything with him. So, too, it is with us. Marriage is a wonderful and blessed vocation and sacrament. But for those called to a celibate priesthood, can anything compare with the riches we are offered? When we come to know some of these riches, we realize that we have only given up a little yet gained a buried treasure in return.

My research study showed that those priests who eventually see their celibate commitment as a calling from God and as a personal grace are the happiest of priests.[8] If we priests become stuck in a negative view of celibacy, seeing it as only an onerous burden and not tasting the riches it offers, then our priesthood cannot really be fully alive and fruitful. Thankfully, my data show that the large majority professes to have found such buried treasure in their celibate commitment. Those who have discovered its riches can only thank God for this unbelievable prefiguring of heaven's blessings.

My brothers, the plain fact is that we are the recipients of blessings so great that if we truly thought about it, it would strain our faith. How could there be a God so generous as to share the fullness of the divine life with us? How could God call a group of men, despite our limitedness and consistent infidelities, to such a gifted life? This generosity can only be explained by love. Love gives of itself completely, fully, and without measure. Let us pray that we priests will respond, however feebly, with our own love. Or rather, may we respond with God's love that dwells in us.

Father, Our love is small. Lean down. Gather us into your arms. Fill us with the infinite riches of your love. May our lives and ministries be filled today and always with you. May we overflow with love for you. And, like you, may we overflow with love for the people you have loved into being. You are love; may we, too, become love.

Becoming Solid People

Dear Brothers,

In my last letter to you, I promised to say something more about prayer. As long as we think of prayer as a task or a duty, it becomes one more burden in our overburdened days. And then it becomes a source of embarrassment and shame. We know we should pray more, but we are just too swamped. We are indeed overfull with tasks. We are just too busy.

I recently received a nice Christmas card from one of my favorite priests, Father Phil Hearn. Phil is a generous pastor who has done much for many people. When I read his cards, I know I am not the shepherd this wonderful man is. Among his many duties, he is the pastor of two parishes, has several elderly priests in his rectory whom he literally cares for, is the bishop's regional vicar, and temporarily took on two more parishes with the unexpected death of another priest. He confided in me he had eighteen funerals in the last two weeks. That's unbelievable. The man willingly accepts all the bishop asks and bravely carries on. And oh, by the way, this exemplary priest is in his seventies! He is a saintly priest.

We have to do something about the workloads of priests today. We are getting older, and there are fewer of us. But the workloads are only increasing. It's not the bishop's fault. If he could make more priests, he certainly would. It's not the fault of priests. It's just the way it is. It is the sign of our times. But it is our responsibility to do something about it.

What does it require? We have to re-vision what it means to be a priest. We cannot continue business as usual without killing our priests. It means we have to begin with the acknowledgment that we priests cannot continue doing all the tasks that our predecessors did. We cannot go to every reception, attend every function, and be available 24/7 as did the great priests before us.

I think the re-visioning process ought to begin with priests sitting down together, with their bishop, and talking, praying, and reflecting. What is the Spirit asking of us today? What are the true needs of our people? What can we realistically do? One priest cannot make the changes by himself; it will take an entire presbyterate, under the leadership of their bishop, to discern and to make it happen.

As a theoretical background, we ought not to fall into the temptation of looking at the Church using a corporate business model. This model, at times, unconsciously drives our actions. We priests are not simply trying to keep the wheels of the organization turning. Rather, we recognize that we are a community of faith guided by the Holy Spirit. We are each, individually and collectively, called to give witness and to serve the people as guided by the Holy Spirit. If we follow the Spirit without reserve, there will be blessings and grace in abundance overflowing for the needs of the community. This is not something a corporation would profess, but it is integral to our vision of Church and Spirit.

This presupposes that we are not simply efficient corporate officers. We are men guided by the Holy Spirit. All the activity in the world is useless unless it is in harmony with God's will. All the activity in the world is insignificant compared to one act done with the infused presence of the Holy Spirit.

You and I have experienced this truth. I am sure there is not one priest reading this letter who has not experienced hearing the still, small voice of God guiding his actions (1 Kgs 19:12). I have heard story upon story: a priest, feeling a "little push" of the Holy Spirit, decides to visit the hospital and finds a person struggling and in need of a priest; a priest about to leave the confessional decides to stay just a moment longer when a man who hasn't been to confession in twenty years stops by at the last moment; or on a whim, a priest calls on a parishioner "just to see how the family is doing" and finds them suffering and in great need. As the years pass and I try ever more diligently to allow the Holy Spirit to direct my life, I can more readily perceive how each seemingly small act has become a moment of meaning and a blessing. When we allow the Spirit to work through us, each of our actions yields much saving grace. When we allow the Spirit to work through us completely, nothing in our lives becomes chance or without purpose.

Prayer opens the conduit for the Spirit to work through us. As we continue to open ourselves to God, we allow God to enter and direct our lives more fully. In prayer, we give ourselves totally to God in love and trust. We have no idea where he will take us. My brothers, did you ever imagine the surprising journey on which God has taken you since the day you prostrated yourself before the altar? We can always be sure that it will be a surprise, although a blessed surprise and a gift.

I remember the day that I decided to let God direct my life. I was in the US Air Force and wondering what I should do with the rest of my life. While having appreciated the air force, I knew it was time for me to move on. There were many options in front of me, and I simply could not figure out which to choose. There were so many unknowns. Who could tell which was best? Who can foresee what is to come? Then it came to me: There is only One who knows what is best. I'll let him guide me, and whatever path he chooses, it must be the best. As they say, "The rest is history." It certainly has been a wild ride. But the wild ride begins with prayer and opening ourselves to God, letting the Spirit fill us and guide us.

Prayer is not so much a thing we do, as if we are sending a letter to God who lives a long way off. It is not primarily an informational session. It is a trusting time of loving intercommunion. This is why "saying prayers" is a good thing, but looking at God in our hearts and loving him is best.

In order for our prayer to be truly Christian, it must recognize that, in the person of Jesus, God has entered our world and our human condition. Prayer is our direct and explicit way of letting God take over our lives, our priesthood, and our hearts. When God directs our lives, we are moving in sync with the divine plan. When God directs our priesthood, we become wonderfully efficacious. When God fills our hearts, we overflow with love for God and for all.

Prayer is especially a divine gift to our celibate priesthood. While all people are given God's riches in prayer, we have a unique union with him in love and predilection. As the years pass, we priests become more aware of our human frailty—the bravado of youth necessarily dissipates with age. As the years pass, we become more aware of how unable we are to accomplish anything without God's Spirit. He is indeed increasing and we are truly decreasing.

Did you ever read C. S. Lewis's short book *The Great Divorce*? If not, you should do so. There are many important truths and striking images conveyed in this work. One image that stands out is how people, as they "descend" into hell, get smaller and more ghostlike until they literally disappear. Their humanity is gone, and there is left but an empty, hollow shell. On the other hand, those who journey increasingly closer to God become larger, stronger, brighter, and more solid. He referred to them as the "solid people," the "bright people," or the "white spirit." When we come closer to God, we become more solid people.

When I do not pray, I feel empty. I feel dried up and hollow. If I were to stop praying altogether, I think

I would become like one of C. S. Lewis's ghosts. I
would become smaller and less human, until I disap-
peared into an empty shell. But as I pray more and
allow God to fill me, I am truly changed. I feel stronger, brighter, and more alive. I feel solid. As the years
pass, I feel ever more needful of prayer and ever more
needful of God. Not only do I feel unable to pass a significant amount of time without praying, but also each
moment I find myself becoming increasingly aware
and open to our God who is always here. More and
more we are making St. Paul's admonition a reality—
to pray always. Each year, God is increasingly in our
consciousness.

This is the prayer of a priest. Of course, we must set
aside specific moments of dedicated prayer each day.
However, throughout the day, the heart and mind of
a priest become increasingly and consciously open to
Love, who is eternally present. As someone wholly dedicated to God, in heart and mind, we become truly his.

This is what God wants of us—everything. And,
this is what we truly want as well—to be solely and
completely his. As we are increasingly filled with God,
the empty ghost that we once were becomes stronger,
more solid, and brighter. This is the enormity of priesthood and the magnificence of our calling. Let no one
deceive you with a priesthood of anything less.

When we become aware of the totality and enormity of this calling, we become aware that we have
fallen short. We are not all that we should be. So,
today, let us begin again. We resolve to let God fill
us with his presence. In prayer, we open ourselves to
divine beauty. Captured by Love and enthralled with

such beauty, let us give ourselves over and completely to him. Finally, eventually, we truly become priests; we become solid people.

⧉

In those days, he departed to the mountain to pray, and he spent the night in prayer to God.

—Luke 6:12

One Holy Priest

Dear Brothers,

Occasionally, this "heretical" thought comes to me: "We do not need more priests; we need only one holy priest." In our day, so much is being said about the need for more priests, which is true enough. But our first need is for holy priests. In the past, we have not had a shortage of priests; we have had too many. When we have had men ill placed in the priesthood, people have suffered. We would prosper with fewer, more holy men.

However, when I look at you, my brothers, I see holy men. I think of the wonderful pastors in my diocese that I have known. As an altar boy, I remember them. In the early years of my priesthood, I was an associate and learned from them. Now, these holy pastors are my peers and friends. No doubt you have such holy men in your diocese as well. They are wonderful role models for younger priests. I admire them; they inspire me.

But I have also worked with other men who could not live priesthood with integrity. I do not know what to say. Their sins have been splashed across the front page of the paper. Nevertheless, they are my brothers and I can truly say I love them. Perhaps I love them a bit more because of their weaknesses. Many of them are filled with shame. It was my great joy and honor to minister to them for seventeen years. Could there be any greater honor than to minister to our brothers, to priests, in their time of need?

I wish others could know them as I have known them. They, too, would love them, despite their sins, although sometimes these were horrendous. Many people wear their friends with status like a badge of honor. "I know so and so," or "So and so is a friend of mine." They are the important people. It has been my privilege to know you, my brothers, and even the least among you. I felt your pain and your failure. Sadly, a few of you took your own lives; the shame was too great.

We cannot lightly excuse your crimes and your sins. You felt the burden. It weighed like a millstone around your neck. I tried to carry it with you, at least a few steps. In the end, it was yours to carry. I would say this to these wounded brothers, the "least" among us: I would rather be in your shoes, despite your great crimes, than to be among the smooth, the sleek, and the arrogant. You have a fighting chance of making it into the kingdom. You have come to realize the enormity of your sins. For you, all that remains is a life of penance. Shouldn't we all be living such a life?

I have been changed because of such days of pain. We have all been changed. I hope it is for the better.

I believe that God will make it so. There are some of the faithful who have left our company; we are sad but we understand. The men who did such awful things were our brothers, so the "sin" is upon us all. We must learn to love the Church, even in its sinfulness; it is the Church that Jesus loves. It was thus even for Peter, whom Jesus once called "Satan" (Mt 16:23).

In each of us priests there is a mixture of all these men. There is the saint in us. We take great pride in it. To our shame, there is also the sinner. This, too, is part of us. Together, the face of the priesthood is the face of humanity. In our humanity, we are a mirror for the people. Sometimes, we are very good. Sometimes, we are average. In some moments, we are bad. But we are always God's people, never abandoned.

We cannot lightly excuse such sins, but we do ask for forgiveness. We do not ask for some cheap grace, as if a word of forgiveness would expunge all the evil done in the world. No, evil causes intense suffering in others and in ourselves. It will take much fire to purify the evil in us. Thank God for Jesus who alone can take on such an impossible task.

God did not choose angels to be priests. We have an obligation to work mightily to purify the priesthood, to winnow it so that it is replete with holy men. But it will always have some, and there are parts of us, too, that are not yet redeemed. These will remind us of the need for a Savior. These will remind us of our flawed humanity, which makes us brothers with the people whom we serve. We are not better than they; we are only their servants.

How can a true priest become an arrogant man? When he sees such weakness in the world and, if he is honest, sees the same human weakness in himself, he can only fall down on his face and ask for mercy. Perhaps some of us have not yet summoned the courage to see the truth. Do we have the courage to face the weakness of the world and our own?

Today's priests should be apostles of the confessional. The fundamental sins of humanity and of the priesthood should drive us all to the confessional. Benedict XVI spoke of this blessed sacrament as one of the keys to renewal. I agree. We must be men of the altar and of the confessional. The true dignity of the priesthood and its true mercy are seen in the midst of weakness and sin. *Ego te absolvo.* No one else can utter those sacramental words but a priest. Then we are reborn in grace.

The pain and suffering of the priesthood in the United States and increasingly around the world these past years has, at times, been excruciating. It has been the result of our own sins. And the evil one has pressed his advantage. Ironically, the very fire that has been visited upon the Church is becoming a refining fire. This suffering is making the priests precisely into what we need to become—holy men.

I would not wish to relive one year of the past decade. I hope that today's younger priests do not have to undergo the same years of trial. But I know better; they will have their own trials. "The cup that I drink, you shall drink" (Mk 10:39). To be a priest means that one must drink of the same cup. The priest who is not nailed to the cross is just another imposter, leading the people astray.

There is no other road to salvation than the Cross. Jesus said, "Come and follow me." May he give us the strength to carry our crosses. May this road lead us to true holiness. People need holy priests. My brothers, I look at your faces, and I see the faces of holy men.

Holiness is not some empty beatific smile and uttering pious platitudes. Holiness is hard won. It is etched into a worn face. Each line corresponds to the lash of years of self-giving service. I can't imagine doing eighteen funerals in two weeks, but only three weeks ago, a priest over seventy years old did them all. Each one of those bereaved parties had no inkling of the burden. As it should have been, they only knew that their loved one had died and that a priest was there to give them comfort.

Perhaps this is all it takes. These are the flashes of greatness. These are the moments of true sanctity and complete self-giving. These are the moments when the true meaning of priesthood is lived out. No one will likely take note or remember, except the One Priest who gave us his life, rejected by the society of his day.

How many priests do we need? We needed only one, Jesus. Today, in him, we have enough. When the sacrifice of Jesus is renewed in but one priest, the entire world is again offered the gift of salvation. When we perform one truly holy act, Christ's sacrifice is again made present. There is no power here or below that can neutralize this saving eucharistic act.

When a priest utters the words, "This is my body; this is my blood," he re-presents the words of Jesus.

He speaks them in his own name and in the name of all the suffering faithful. As a priest, his own blood is in that cup and his body is broken for the people. In that cup and on that plate are the sufferings of all. Then, for him and for them, it is consummated. *Consummatum est*. Then, as it was for Jesus, he can say, "It is finished."

A Narcissistic Minefield

My Brothers,

I recently read some disturbing news. Studies of young people suggest that narcissism is increasing rapidly in this country and has been doing so since the 1970s. While there are critiques of these studies, a societal increase in narcissism (an excessive egocentrism) has a ring of truth to it. Actually, given the rising secularity, I think it is inevitable. When God is dismissed from one's life equation, then the human person and the self are all that is left. Then all the "planets" revolve around the earth, rather than the Son. We have placed ourselves at the center of the universe. Unfortunately, human beings are not up to the task. It is the ultimate narcissistic act.

Priests are not immune from the pathology of the day. We come from a culture and a context. It is very hard to separate ourselves from all of the cultural distortions around us. Each society promotes a specific spectrum of pathology in individuals based upon its collective pathology. For example, Victorian England was known for its emotional inhibition, including an inhibited sexuality. Some would suggest that this inhibited society spawned widespread hysterical disorders, as they were then called. On the other hand, today's secularity is spawning widespread narcissism. In today's society we priests are naturally infected with the narcissism "virus" to a greater or lesser extent.

In addition, priesthood itself can be a minefield for the potential narcissist. Within only a couple of years after ordination, we become pastors of parishes. We become the boss. Of course, most subordinates are naturally deferential to their bosses. The young priest, with narcissistic tendencies, can end up being "king" of the parish. When we celebrate the Sunday Masses, we are dressed up and preside over the congregation. These can be narcissistic field days for those so inclined. For some, the Mass becomes more about them than it does about Jesus. Having the spotlight shining on us can make the best of us prone to a touch of self-congratulatory praise.

Not having a spouse is also an occasion to promote narcissism, which can include an unrealistic appraisal of one's self. There is nothing like a spouse who lives with a person day and night for years to provide an objective opinion and needed feedback. It is part of any healthy marriage for spouses to correct each other and to keep one another grounded in reality. Often I hear a spouse give just the right pinprick to deflate the narcissistic "hot air" in their mates.

If we priests become isolated, "full of ourselves," and unwilling to take in feedback, narcissism can run unchecked in our psyches. Narcissistic men increasingly surround themselves with people who applaud them and actually fuel their self-adulation. Narcissists are often surrounded by groupies who reinforce their feelings of being exceptional and above the law. This is not just true for priesthood; there are many walks of life that can attract and inflame narcissists. These are especially found in the public arena where individuals are given power and public attention. Public leaders who succumb to narcissism are ripe for a fall.

Dean Ludwig and Clinton Longenecker, professors of management, describe the Bathsheba Syndrome, in which successful, upper-level managers may come to see themselves, like King David, as above the rules.[9] In their vulnerable state, these leaders may lose a sense of propriety and judgment and become prone to ethical violations. One need not look far to see examples of successful public leaders who have become involved in sordid affairs that ruined their brilliant careers. Their lives became narcissistically inflated and eventually the pinprick came that deflated all the hot air of their accumulated hubris.

There are few checks on a priest's authority and leadership. Parish councils can easily become ineffective under the reign of a narcissistic pastor. Chancery officials usually have little ability to moderate such a man's leadership. A personal intervention by the bishop can be effective, but these are difficult to orchestrate and are a last-ditch strategy.

Narcissism is the very antithesis of priesthood. Priestly life is about service and self-giving. The narcissist is about "me" and "my needs." A little self-care is healthy and, in proportion, makes a life of self-giving possible. The narcissist, on the other hand, loses his focus on the other and his entire world becomes about himself. He may rationalize it by saying that what is best for him is best for the parish.

I saw a frightening video on YouTube. It was a short clip in which a fairly young priest gave witness to a near-death experience that he had. He was in a car accident and "died." He was being judged by Our Lord who condemned him to hell because "he has been a priest for twelve years for himself and not for me." In his own words, he took the easy way out and never preached the hard truths needed today. Fortunately, our Blessed Mother interceded for him, and he was given a second chance.

Such near-death experiences are, of course, not *de fide* but rather fall into the area of private revelations. We are not obligated to believe such stories, but I found that this one had the ring of truth to it and was very much in line with our Catholic theology. It might seem hard to believe until we recognize that narcissism is the antithesis of priesthood and of the Gospel. The priest had fallen into a narcissistic lifestyle, having served "twelve years for himself." We ought to remember that the supreme narcissist is Satan whose kingdom is one of total self-focus. Such narcissism can never know the saving mystery of true love.

What is the antidote to the frightening possibility this priest encountered? First, we ought to begin by listening. We take the focus off ourselves and listen to those around us, to the Church, and to our God. When we truly listen, we find out who the people are and what they need. When we listen to the Church, we find out the whole truth that we are to preach and teach. When we listen to God, we learn the true nature of love.

Second, after listening, we prostrate ourselves before God and the Church and say, "Thy will be done." The prostration of a priest at his ordination is a wonderful symbol of the self-emptying that is essential to priesthood. Each morning when I get up, I say the prayer of Brother Charles de Foucauld that begins, "Father, I abandon myself into your hands; do with me what you will."

Third, when we fall, we ourselves go to confession and ask forgiveness. We, too, are reminded that we are sinners without hope were it not for Jesus. No one is saved without him. "There is no salvation through anyone else, nor is there any other name under heaven given to the human race by which we are to be saved" (Acts 4:12). Our mission as priests is first and foremost the salvation of souls. Our goal is to introduce them to Jesus. In the sacraments and in all of our ministrations, we endeavor to help make the Savior present and alive in people's lives. "He must increase, I must decrease" (Jn 3:30).

My brothers, unchecked narcissism is the road to destruction. Our secular society has made man the center of the universe, and thus it promotes man to a role that he cannot fulfill. Without God, we cannot find our true humanity. Without God, our countenance is disfigured, and if unchecked, it is destroyed.

The antidote is mere Christianity. We listen, we prostrate ourselves in service, we learn to love our fellow men and women, and thus we learn to love God.

You and I have a privileged role in the economy of salvation. But we ought never forget that we are first Christians and thus we too must walk the road that Jesus walked. We walk that road by being true priests, men of service to God, the Church, and the people around us, where we work out our own salvation.

Because we have been given so much, much more is expected and needed. There are many souls who will not hear the saving Word if we do not preach it. We ought not to miss one opportunity to be a source of grace for others. We long to "squeeze" every possible drop of grace out of our lives before the Lord calls us home. We long to give "the last full measure of our devotion."

Is this beyond us? In my diocese, there are over thirty priests who are beyond retirement age who still voluntarily remain pastors in full-time priestly service. No one would fault them for retiring to a comfortable life in a warmer climate. God knows we all fantasize about it. I suspect they have as well. But they remain in our parishes. The diocese would be in very difficult straits were it not for these generous old men. We even have one priest, now eighty-seven years of age, serving as the pastor and only priest in a large parish.

These priests are giving the last full measure of their devotion. They are "squeezing" the last drop of grace out of their lives before the end. Can there be any doubt about their destiny beyond death? We learn from them. We are inspired by them. We thank God for them. I can only conclude that we are living in a time of holy priests.

After withdrawing about a stone's throw from them and kneeling, he prayed, saying, "Father, If you are willing, take this cup away from me; still, not my will but yours be done." And to strengthen him an angel from heaven appeared to him.

—Luke 22:41–43

The Ultimate Choice

Dear Brothers,

Today, I offered Mass for deceased priests. We are brothers in life . . . and in death. There is a saying often attributed to St. John Chrysostom: "The road to hell is paved with the bones of priests and monks, and the skulls of bishops are the lamp posts that light the path." This is a bit dour. However, there is no doubt in my mind that some of our deceased (and living) brothers desperately need our prayers and our support. If you have a Mass without an intention, you too might offer it for our brothers.

I remember once doing a psychological and spiritual evaluation of a priest who had been involved in many twisted sexual liaisons as well as other disturbing behaviors. He had long since ceased praying. At the end of the evaluation, I sat down privately with him and his bishop. I summarized the situation with a stark and direct statement, and the bishop understood its import. I looked at the priest and said, "You are going down the wrong path." Sadly, the man had no visible response.

On a smaller scale, there are more than a few of our brothers who are caught up in the destructive web of Internet pornography. This is a cancer on our society and, sadly, among some of our seminarians and priests as well. A few others are involved in frequent sexual liaisons, alcohol or drug addiction, or are self-absorbed in their own wants and desires. This is not the stuff of heaven. When priests die in such a state, we pray that, at least, they enter a time of purgation rather than be lost forever.

You and I ought never to presume upon God's mercy. Just because we are priests, we ought not to presume that we are among the elect. In fact, the bar for us is higher. We have been given many graces; we are expected to respond in generosity. We do not want to be the ones who pound on the gates of heaven saying, "Lord, open the door for us," only to hear in response, "I do not know where you are from" (Lk 13:25).

When I think of such things, it frightens me a bit. I think I am in good company. In his sermon "On Pastors," St. Augustine said he will come to God not only as a Christian but also as a leader. Thus, he said, he bears a heavier burden. "I as a leader must give him an account of my stewardship as well." St. Augustine said, "I must listen with fear and trembling."[10] A pious exaggeration? I think not. It is a holy fear.

Before the Second Vatican Council, we felt fortunate if we squeaked into purgatory. In our day, it is often suggested that everyone will be saved. In reality, we do not know how many will be saved. That knowledge is reserved to God alone. But we do know, *de fide*, that hell exists as a real possibility. Jesus himself said, "The gate is wide and the road broad that leads to destruction, and those who enter through it are many. How narrow the gate and constricted the road that leads to life. And those who find it are few" (Mt 7:13–14). The scriptures, the tradition of the Church, and the witness of the saints consistently indicate that more than a few have chosen the darkness.

We should make no mistake about it. There are many scriptural references to a place of damnation where there will be "wailing and grinding of teeth" (Lk 13:28). We priests do not want to return to the old days of hellfire and brimstone preaching, trying to scare people into being good. We have found, ultimately, that this does not work. People are best drawn to the love of God and the sweetness of his mercy.

Nevertheless, we do people a disservice if we never speak of the four last things: death, judgment, heaven, and hell. These are uncomfortable truths. We preach a Gospel that, at times, is uncomfortable. We squirm a bit when we reflect upon such things. This is good. If we do not squirm a bit when the thought of hell enters our minds, then we really do not understand.

The choices that you and I make in life have real and eternal consequences. We do not take seriously enough the gift of free will that God has given to us. This free will allows us to choose. Since we can really choose, we can really love. Each time we choose the good, we are choosing to love.

But we can also choose evil. If we choose evil, then we will reap its very real consequences. We only need to look at the world around us to realize that choosing evil is something that is done much more than people would like to admit.

We priests are not to stand apart from such things, futilely trying to wash our hands as Pilate tried to do. We need to wade into the darkness of the world. As Jesus descended into hell, you and I must enter the world of sinners. Of course, I am not speaking of us intentionally sinning. Rather we ought to face directly all the ugliness of the world and bring to it the Author of Light. We recognize the growing darkness around us and raise the alarm. At the same time, we offer the path of light to those who will accept it.

This is why our ministry in the confessional is so important. The world is wallowing in darkness. God reaches into the darkness in the person of Jesus and offers people a way out. The confessional is one of the most powerful means that we are given. How many penitents have you and I heard who shed tears of relief during a heartfelt confession? As a psychologist, I can do much good by listening and working with clients. But as a priest in the confessional, we can do immensely more. No one else can sacramentally forgive sin in the name of Jesus and be such an instrument of God's healing grace.

In our day, we are losing a sense of sin. Thus we are losing a sense of the need to confess. Priests are being replaced by psychotherapists. And in the modern consciousness, the specter of hell recedes into a seeming anachronism. We have created a more comfortable world for ourselves. Unfortunately, the witness of scripture and the consistent tradition of faith teach a different truth. It reminds me of a terrific line from the movie *City of Angels*, when the doctor said to the angel, "I don't believe in that." The angel responded, "Some things are true whether you believe in them or not."

On the other hand, it would also be a mistake to get stuck reflecting only on the reality of hell. This feeds the darkness. My parents once chaffed at a monsignor whose only homily week after week was a negative, hellfire message. An occasional acknowledgment of sin and hell is important. More than that suggests some obsessional thinking that may say more about the preacher than the parishioner.

As priests, while acknowledging the darkness, we turn our eyes to the light. We recognize the possibility of hell, but we turn our attention to heaven. The eyes of the saints are focused on the radiant beauty of God.

This reminds me of how crucial the life of a priest is. We traffic in the things of ultimate importance. People are ecstatic, as they should be, when a medical doctor intervenes and "saves" their lives. Eventually, however, they will die. On the other hand, the priest intervenes so that they might be saved forever. When people lose a sense of a real heaven and a real hell, a living God and real evil, then the priest becomes irrelevant, at best a kind of pious social worker. If we lose a sense of the ongoing temptations and real devastation of sin, then we have no need of a man who can be a conduit for God's forgiveness and his strengthening grace.

When you and I stand among the people, our presence ought to bring to people's mind all these realities.

When they see us, dressed in our religious or clerical garb, they are reminded of a God who loves them. They should also be reminded of the real possibility of evil. Our joyful faces ought to remind them of the true joy that God offers, and conversely the possibility of the anguish of eternal darkness. Is it any wonder that people react so strongly to us?

We have all had the experience of strangers spontaneously greeting us with affection and a big smile. We have also had the experience of a stranger's disdain and hostility. What we represent ought to bring out people's strongest emotions, and it does. Much of our preaching is simply being present among the people of this divided world. Seeing us, they are reminded of their fundamental choice. Some would like to distance themselves from this choice, but they cannot. Not to choose is to choose poorly. "Whoever is not with me is against me, and whoever does not gather with me scatters" (Lk 11:23).

Our presence ought to remind people that, despite the pressures of this world, they can choose the good and live a graced life. It is possible and there is help. We invite them into our communities where people of faith can support each other and where their saving faith can be nourished. We invite them in, and we daily labor to build up these communities of faith. They are havens for us humans who are so vulnerable. Together, we are stronger.

This is what a good shepherd does. You are those good shepherds. Is it any wonder that the forces of darkness want to destroy you? But we are safe in God's house. We minister under the watchful eye of our

Mother and in the name of her Son. The Spirit encircles us in love and peace. We are protected.

See, I have today set before you life and good, death and evil. If you obey the commandments of the Lord, your God, which I am giving you today, loving the Lord, your God, and walking in his ways . . . you will live and . . . the Lord, your God, will bless you.

—Deuteronomy 30:15–26

Parish Priest as Exorcist

My Brothers,

Have you heard about the possessed woman in the confessional who was speaking to the Curé of Ars? She was overheard saying, "Without that [blasphemous term to refer to our Lady] who is up above, we should have you for certain; but she protects you, together with that great dragon [St. Michael] who is at the door of your church."[11]

We can try to dismiss the witness of St. John Vianney, the patron of priests, by relegating him in our minds to one of those "medieval saints." We think their day was very different and so long ago that it is hard for us to relate. But it was actually only a bit more than 150 years ago that this saintly priest died. My house is almost that old. The Curé of Ars is a modern saint for our time and for us.

If you have trouble believing in the existence of a personified evil, just reread only a little bit of his life. The demons tormented him regularly. Some of the other diocesan priests didn't believe it until they slept in the same building with him one evening. They found out differently. The devil referred to the Curé as an "ugly black toad." Satan hates priests and he especially hated St. John Vianney.

There are some people out there who hate us. There are organizations that hate the Church and are out to destroy it. At times, we have deserved the disdain we have received because of our sins. But there are some people and organizations that we should not want to like us. At the top of the list is the devil and all those who do his bidding, consciously or unconsciously. Priests are definitely in the devil's crosshairs.

The issue of exorcisms is recently coming back into consciousness among the faithful and among the leaders of the Church. Secular society treats the subject as an oddity that sells movies and magazines. The subject is surrounded with so much abuse and distortion that it is little wonder that more than a few priests keep the subject at arm's length. Sometimes we priests have been our own worst enemies in dealing with this ministry. But our priestly ministry is an implicit, if not sometimes explicit, exorcism.

Our faith teaches us that, because of human sin, creation fell under the sway of the devil. Before baptism, the person has not yet been redeemed. Baptism is not simply a pious exercise to celebrate a birth. It wrestles a soul from the clutches of death and brings it into God's saved family. It is a critical moment in the life of every soul and thus a solemn and important ministry of the priest. We should not let the cake, the flowers, all the preparations, and the niceties obscure in our minds, or in the people's minds, exactly what happens in this pivotal sacrament.

During the baptism, the priest performs a "minor" exorcism. He asks the questions, "Do you renounce Satan? And all his works? And all his empty promises?" I prefer to use this option, which is a bit more direct about the exorcism that is occurring. It is good to know that what we are renouncing is not simply an abstract lifestyle or sin in general but also a real being. In this sacrament, the soul moves out of the darkness and into the light of Christ.

When we baptize, as when we hear confessions and preside at the Eucharist, we are bringing souls to Christ and out of the grip of evil. Is it any wonder the devil hates priests? And since the demons are preternatural beings, they have preternatural power, speed, and knowledge—more than we slow, dull, and weak humans. For once Satan spoke the truth when he told the Curé that he would "have him for certain" were it not for the Blessed Mother and St. Michael. By ourselves, we are no match for the devil. Unfortunately, a few exorcists have found this out the hard way. They forgot it was Christ's power that casts out the devil, having relied on their own.

But like St. John Vianney, we should not be afraid, because Our Lady protects us, and St. Michael and the legions of angels are our allies, not to mention the all-powerful holy name of Jesus. We should never hesitate to ask for help. After one such encounter in the past with evil, I am never without my rosary beads in my pocket, which I often thumb. A healthy fear of the powers of darkness and a loving trust in this beautiful woman should be part of every priest's armament.

Dioceses do not receive many cases of true possession. Be assured there are some. Yet the daily influence of the demonic in people's lives is real. You provide people with the means to remain safe and to travel down the path to holiness. What should you do and recommend for those who have some ongoing encounter with evil? The answer is pretty much the same as for those seeking to live a holy life:

- Frequent the sacraments often, including the Eucharist and the Sacrament of Penance.
- Pray often, invoking the intercession of Our Lady, especially in the rosary; the intercession of the saints; and the aid of St. Michael and the angels.
- Have a priest bless the people and their houses including every room.
- Put up crosses in the house and liberally use holy water.
- Reject all sin and pray.

Also, if there is some opening through which the demonic entered a person's life, this ought to be exposed and explicitly renounced. For example, if the person began to invoke the spirits of the dead or became involved in the occult, he or she ought to renounce explicitly these evil actions. Not only does the person renounce the figure of Satan, repeating the baptismal rite, but also he or she ought to renounce any and all evil practices and sins by name. Just as it is important to name and reject our sins in the confessional, so too is it important to do so in a prayer for deliverance.

Cases of full possession are to be referred to the bishop. But the first "exorcists" in a diocese are not the ones appointed by the bishop to perform a solemn exorcism. The first exorcists are the priests on the front lines confronting evil every day and bringing people to Jesus Christ.

The parish priest is "armed" with the weapons of light. In fact, the majority of what a designated exorcist uses in a solemn exorcism is part of the daily "weapons" of every priest. You and I pray in the name of Jesus. We bless people with holy water and hold up the cross for veneration. We invoke Mary and all the saints in their various litanies. We pray to St. Michael to "defend us in battle." We lay our hands on people's heads and invoke the Holy Spirit. You, my brothers, are frontline agents in the fight against evil and exorcising demons in the holy name of Jesus.

St. John Vianney was just such a parish priest. The devil complained, "You have taken more than 80,000 souls from me."[12]

As noted, it is tempting for those involved in this priestly ministry to be prideful. The seventy-two returned to Jesus and said, "Lord, even the demons are subject to us because of your name." Jesus cautioned, "I have observed Satan fall like lightning from the sky. Behold, I have given you the power to tread . . . upon the full force of the enemy and nothing will harm you. Nevertheless, do not rejoice because the spirits are subject to you, but rejoice because your names are written in heaven" (Lk 10:17–20).

Could this scripture passage be any clearer? You and I are given the power and the duty to cast out demons. But most importantly, our eyes should be fixed on heaven. Evil is not to be trifled with, but we ought not to give it more due than it is worth. Satan is a pitiable creature and powerless in the presence of Jesus. We rejoice because we priests are sons of God and images of Jesus. We have a most holy woman who watches over us and the Holy Spirit who infuses and guides us.

When we think of such things, the words of the Psalmist spring to mind.

And so, my heart rejoices, my soul is glad;
even my flesh shall rest in hope.
For you will not abandon my soul to hell,
nor let your holy one see corruption.
You will show me the path of life,
the fullness of joy in your presence,
at your right hand, bliss forever.
                    —Revised Grail Psalter 16:9–11

Be Brothers!

My Brothers,

I was speaking with an older bishop recently, and he was reminiscing about his life. He said, "I would never have made it without my brother priests." He spoke about his early days in the priesthood and how challenging they were. He had a rough time with one particularly difficult pastor, and he said it was the support from his priest friends that got him through. Even now, as a bishop, he relies heavily on his priest friends.

A priest without any priest friends is an oddity. There are a few, but it is an unnatural life. All of us priests should also have good lay friends, and most do, which is very important. A totally isolated priest will never live priesthood quite right. There will always be problems; the full flowering of a priestly life in isolation is just not possible.

As a psychologist, I often speak to priests about the importance of friends and human relationships. Today, this is so commonly spoken of in priestly screening and formation as to be a given. I think young seminarians in the United States are a bit tired of hearing it. And I hear no one in authority arguing the point of its importance.

But the issue of the critical need for human relationships is deeper than simply being good for one's psyche. It points to a reality that often escapes our individualistic, Western minds. In countries like the United States, we have grown accustomed to growing up in isolated, nuclear families (or broken families) and striking off on our own in adulthood. In fact, being self-sufficient is a source of pride for Americans.

Such an approach would be unthinkable in many cultures. When I was in Mexico, I lived with a family for several weeks. Next door lived a brother and sister-in-law. Down the street were two of the children and their families. Around the corner were aunts and uncles. In fact, the entire extended family lived close to each other and daily walked in and out of each other's homes. Suggesting to them that they separate from the extended family and live by themselves would have been met with incredulity.

In our American rugged individuality we have lost a sense of the communal. Unity and communion are an essential part of being human. Of course, for Christianity, unity and communion are especially essential concepts and carry a deeply theological significance as well. To be Christian is to be part of a communion of brothers and sisters, united to our God. Whatever breaks this communion must be called a sin.

This is why pope after pope in our modern era has spoken about the importance of Christian unity. It is not just a pious, secondary thought. Rather, it is part of the very nature of the Body of Christ and the task of every Christian. Jesus prayed for it fervently:

> "That they may all be one, as you, Father, are in me and I in you, that they also may be in us, that the world may believe that you sent me. And I have given them the glory you gave me, so that they may be one, as we are one, I in them and you in me, that they may be brought to perfection" (Jn 17:21–23).

In this clear and forceful passage, Jesus is praying that we all might be one because he and the Father are one. Our communion mirrors the perfection of God. As God is one, so we should be one. Thus, we are "brought to perfection."

We Christians strive for unity because it is part of our nature and our perfection. People will not believe the Good News unless they see this unity. As the scripture quote says, "That the world may believe." Truly, the disunity among Christians is a scandal to the world and an obstacle to its belief in Jesus.

We priests must be the first ones to promote Christian unity. A significant part of that is the unity of priests. How can we priests possibly promote Christian unity when we can't get along ourselves? When I travel from diocese to diocese, the first concern I hear from priests is about workloads. There is too much to do. The second concern I hear is about priestly unity. Priests themselves are not satisfied with the current state of disharmony.

In my research, I asked priests about many things— delineating sources of happiness and unhappiness. An area that received some of the worst scores was priests supporting each other. Of great concern were the divisions among priests today: young versus old, liberal versus conservative, or "Vatican II" priests versus "orthodox" priests. The divide is wide, and the moat in between seemingly uncrossable. For anyone who tries, his credentials are questioned by his peers.

In an earlier letter, I wrote to you about the pathology of a culture subtly affecting the people, including our priests. I suspect that the divisions in priesthood today are an echo and a reflection of the sharp divisions among Americans. The separation of "red states" and "blue states" is divisive, and politics on the national level have become dysfunctional. Our elected officials cannot agree on basic principles, and they have been unable to pass needed legislation. The government is in danger of grinding to a halt.

On the other hand, there are moments when our priestly unity shines out. A few years ago, it was my silver jubilee year of ordination, and as it turns out, I was unable to celebrate this occasion as I had hoped. I was disappointed. However, some weeks later, I was in a diocese speaking at its convocation, and it turned out that they were honoring silver jubilarians. They had a special Mass and gave each the gift of a commemorative stole. They found out I, too, was celebrating twenty-five years and more than welcomed me among them. It was a lovely celebration. I still cherish the stole and wear it as a reminder. Such moments remind me, brothers, of your love and your care. Such moments remind me of our loving God.

My brothers, I offer three concepts that might help strengthen our communion. They are concepts I hold to and they help me. Perhaps they can be of help to you.

First, Catholic theology has always been about "both/and" rather than "either/or." One of the geniuses of Catholic theology has always been its sensitivity to the complexities of life. Authentic Catholic theological statements are always nuanced. When we read the theological works of St. Thomas Aquinas, we quickly see how the Angelic Doctor incorporates a variety of little truths, sometimes seemingly contradictory, into a complex and masterful exposition of the one truth. If Thomas had lived in our day, he would have incorporated ideas of the Right and the Left, liberal and conservative, into a weaving of a fuller exposition of the truth.

I find that the important theological points of the Right and the Left always have some truths in them that are truly Catholic. John Stuart Mill is quoted as saying, "In all intellectual debates, both sides tend to be correct in what they affirm, and wrong in what they deny."[13] I find it so with many of the debates today. What they affirm has some theological truth in them. When they condemn the "others," they often paint a caricature that they then skewer.

One way forward today is to recognize that the principles and ideas that our brother priests so passionately fight for have some important Catholic truths in them that we need to honor and support. It does not mean we must agree with everything, but rather we support and acknowledge whatever we find to be authentically Christian and Catholic. But that implies a certain openness to listening to our brothers and not summarily dismissing them.

The second point that I find helpful is to recognize the need for unity in diversity. There is always a danger in believing that one's own portrayal of the faith is the only accurate one. While there are dogmas to be sure, how one speaks of such eternal truths in the varied cultures of the day will take on varied faces. These multiform presentations of the one truth, when done with integrity, do not detract but actually are required. We cannot do justice to the truth unless we come at it from many directions. The beauty of God is like a many-faceted crystal. Each facet needs to be expounded, and when all put together, the whole radiates the divine truth.

Just so it is with the priesthood. There is not one way of being a priest, although there are bedrock beliefs upon which priesthood is built. We need all of our brothers to show us a complete face of the priesthood. There are pastors, theologians, chaplains, and administrators. We have popes, archbishops, bishops, and priests. We have liberals, conservatives, moderates, pragmatists, consensus builders, prophets, and pastoral men. Some work in the Vatican; others work with the poor in the inner cities.

All of these men together show us a more complete face of priesthood. We need each other. By ourselves, priesthood is incomplete. And God forbid that all of the other priests should be just like us! But all of us together complete the face of priesthood. Our true unity can only be found in our diversity.

Finally, the third concept is to understand my brother priest, especially his background and his life experiences that have brought him to where he is today. For example, I may or may not like liberation theology, but I suspect that if I grew up in an oppressive culture and witnessed the tortures and sufferings of the people, as many of them have, I might be very open to some of the truths embedded in this theology.

Likewise, it is my firm conviction that if the "Vatican II" priests grew up in today's culture, rather than in the 1940s and 1950s, they would be a lot like the young priests of today, and vice versa. I have spent a lot of time with the young "orthodox" priests of today, and they have had to fight against the pressures of today's secularist culture, to profess their faith, and to enter into the priesthood. Is it little wonder that they insist on wearing their clerics, proudly profess to be Catholics, and hold to a strong theological understanding of the Church's teaching? They are fighting to profess and spread the faith that they rightly perceive to be under attack. I believe that most of the "Vatican II" priests, if they had grown up today, would be much like these young priests.

Similarly, if the young priests of today had grown up in the era before the Second Vatican Council, they too would likely be ardent supporters of the Council and its much needed reforms. They would rejoice in the outpouring of the Spirit in the Second Vatican Council and remain its proponents. Many of these hard-won reforms are taken for granted by the young priests of today. However, these critical reforms came only after decades of struggle. Our life experiences and the needs of the day shape how we experience and express our faith and our priesthood.

In truth, we need both young priests and old priests. We need both the "Vatican II" priests and the "orthodox" priests. Each of these groups brings a perspective and a grace that the priesthood and the Church needs. At the same time, we need each other to moderate our occasional misplaced enthusiasm. We priests are fallible and are not always completely correct. Together, we form a Church that is more Catholic and more faithful to the entire Gospel.

You and I are not called to believe everything a brother tells us. But we are called to love our brothers and to listen to them. For their sake and ours, and for the Church, let us begin by listening to our brothers. When we understand their journeys, sometimes painful, and their hard-won faith, we can only admire them and thank God that we have such faith-filled men.

I do thank you, my brothers. I recognize how hard it truly has been for you to be faithful. I understand the challenge it has been for you to walk each day as a priest in this world. The priesthood and the Church need your witness. I need your witness. The Spirit speaks through you. May God give us the wisdom to hear the truth that you tell and to give thanks to God for you always.

But I say to you, whoever is angry with his brother will be liable to judgment, and whoever says to his brother, "Raqa," will be answerable to the

Sanhedrin, and whoever says, "You fool," will be liable to fiery Gehenna.

—Matthew 5:22

Love the Church

Dear Brothers,

As the years pass, our love for the Church ought to deepen. The Church becomes more to us than a bunch of buildings or a long-cherished history. Today, it is a living organism founded by Jesus and filled with the Spirit. It is in this Church that we were born again in Baptism, and it is in this Church that the Spirit was transmitted personally to us. In this Church, we receive the true Body and Blood of Jesus each day. In this Church, the grace of the first apostles was handed down and we participate directly in that line of grace through our ordination to the priesthood. The full revelation and presence of Jesus is alive today in us, the Church.

However, at one point or another in our journey of priesthood, our love for the Church will be challenged. For example, not too long ago, I heard of a bishop who retired. He had worked hard for over fifty years in the priesthood and episcopacy. Then his replacement came. For some reason, perhaps unintentionally, the new bishop treated the retired man somewhat poorly. The man was cast aside. There is no one more powerless in a diocese than a retired bishop, as this man found out.

I felt bad for him. He did not deserve it. Yet he has kept up a brave countenance, and no one knows of his private sufferings. But I suspect he would rather be thrown into jail by the secular authorities than treated with disdain by the "Church" he has loved for fifty years.

Insiders in Vatican politics tell of this or that cardinal falling out of favor and being cast off to an assignment far from the center of power. So, too, with dioceses who receive new bishops. Those priests once in power can fall out of favor, and a new group gradually emerges. Is it any different in parishes? The faithful director of religious education or parish staff member waits in trepidation for the arrival of the new pastor. She or he hopes not to be one of the casualties of a new leadership. And, so it goes.

Throughout all such machinations, feelings often get bruised, if not downright lacerated. For similar reasons, some bishops are wary of making monsignors. The old saying goes, "When one priest gets the red, nine get the blues." I suspect a cardinal who falls out of favor is equally crushed when he believes the pope no longer favors him and he is cast out of the "inner circle." Our egos are so very frail.

You and I would love Church leaders to recognize and praise us. It is very human to want our father figures to support and favor us. As a psychologist, I recognize this as a universal human dynamic. I must admit, whenever I receive a nice letter from my bishop, my smile is a bit broader that day and my step a little lighter. Is there anyone among us immune to such human foibles?

I spent six years in the US Air Force as an intelligence officer. I heard the expression, "Ninety-nine atta-boys are wiped out by one 'Oh rats!'" (insert saltier language for the real air force expression!). The saying meant that you could do ninety-nine projects very well, but if you messed up one thing, your career was over. I suspect many a bishop has had his episcopal career truncated by one false move. It is true for priests as well. Find yourself on the wrong side of one theological conflict and you could end up on the outs. We are often not kind to our brothers in such circumstances.

It is sad to say, but such political machinations are too often true. The Church not only is a divinely founded and divinely inspired living organism, but also is concretely manifested in a very human organization. And it suffers from all the weaknesses that any large human institution has. In that regard, I do not think we are much different from IBM, GE, or the air force.

Perhaps it is good for us to be cast aside. Did Jesus end his career in a plush retirement position? There is little better training in humility than to be cast aside by the very Church one has served for a score of years. More than a few saints suffered mightily at the hands of Church leaders. In more than a few instances, the Church has contributed to the making of its own saints.

I find Jesus' words so very helpful here: "Take the lowest place" (Lk 14:10). Can we not see this as a direct counterbalance to the narcissism of today? It is part of the entitlement culture of today to believe that we are special and that we deserve to be treated better than others. Do we deserve better than we are receiving? Recall again another saying of Jesus: "When you have done all you have been commanded, say, 'We are unprofitable servants; we have done what we were obliged to do'" (Lk 17:10).

If you and I take the lowest place and truly believe we are "unprofitable servants," then so much of the political machinations of the institutional Church would disappear on every level from the parish right up to the Roman curia. At this very moment, you and I are receiving much, much more than we deserve, solely because of God's generosity. When we recognize this, narcissism turns into gratitude.

Perhaps this thought is a bit naive. But Jesus calls us to it, and we ought to strive mightily to follow his words and his example. He entered into Jerusalem on a donkey. He lived like a poor man. He sought no position of power. He simply told the truth, whether it was convenient or inconvenient. You know where it got him. Jesus specifically addressed the dangers of power and leadership. His words deserve to be quoted at length:

> But Jesus summoned them and said, "You know that the rulers of the Gentiles lord it over them, and the great ones make their authority over them felt. But it shall not be so among you. Rather, whoever wishes to be great among you shall be your servant; whoever wishes to be first among you shall be your slave. Just so, the Son of Man did not come to be

served but to serve and to give his life as a ransom for many." (Mt 20:25–28)

No one celebrates losing the Super Bowl. I often wonder, "What's wrong with being the second best team in football?" That should be an honor. Or how about the man who came in second in the Masters golf tournament in Augusta? When the press interviews him, they always ask him what he did wrong. However, I am thinking, "The man must be a wonderful golfer on top of his game to come in second in the Masters."

We are men and we men typically like to be in positions of power. We have a natural competitive spirit and we want to win. A little healthy competition is a good thing. But it can easily and, often does, get out of control.

Unfortunately, the Church is not immune to such human weaknesses, and they affect us priests, some more than others. The emotional lacerations that we suffer sometimes come from the very humanness of the Church, and they come from our own humanness as well. To transcend this, we ought to remind ourselves who it is that we serve. Ultimately, it is Jesus whom we serve and the people. We poor bishops and priests do what we can, but we ought to have no illusions about the limits of our sanctity. Thank God that Jesus is in charge!

And so, we do love the Church. Each day, the Holy Spirit breathes life into it. Each day, we do our best to be good shepherds. Sometimes I embarrass myself at how poorly I do it. It's a good thing the people are patient. They remind me of how patient our God is with us.

We do love the Church, warts and all. We priests are exceedingly grateful that God loves us, despite our embarrassing weaknesses. We are so blessed to be Catholics. We are doubly blessed to be priests. Jesus suffered and died for this Church. He suffered and died for us. May we priests have the grace to do the same.

And so I say to you, you are Peter, and upon this rock I will build my church, and the gates of the netherworld shall not prevail against it. I will give you the keys to the kingdom of heaven. Whatever you bind on earth shall be bound in heaven; and whatever you loose on earth shall be loosed in heaven.

—Matthew 16:18–19

Catching Fire

My Brothers,

Yesterday, I heard Cardinal Wuerl speak about the New Evangelization. He was certainly on fire with this topic. He has been a champion of the New Evangelization for quite some time and recently returned from the synod in Rome on this topic. No doubt, it will remain a focal point of his ministry for the rest of his life.

Good thing or bad thing? You and I tend to treat the subject like one more program that comes down from on high. We expect to do it for a year or two and then move on to the next program. But I suggest to you, my brothers, that there is something different about this one. It is not just one program among others.

The New Evangelization began to be emphasized by John Paul II years ago, and Benedict XVI continued to push it forward. In fact, Benedict saw the New Evangelization as one of the main focal points of his pontificate. After all, he came from a country where the practice of the faith had greatly diminished. He knew the reality firsthand. Pope Francis has also emphasized the importance of the New Evangelization, not only for the spreading of the Gospel, but also for the health of the Church itself: "When the Church does not come out of herself to evangelize, she becomes self-referent and then she gets sick. The evils that over the course of time happen in ecclesial institutions have their root in a self-reference and a sort of theological narcissism."[14]

In his talk, Cardinal Wuerl spoke of the New Evangelization as not simply another program but rather a lens through which we view the world and the entire ministry of the Church. It should inform everything we do. He also added that he believes this to be an authentic call of the Holy Spirit. The cardinal believes that it is God himself who is now asking this of us.

The cardinal is always a fine speaker and an excellent theologian. His homilies are theologically balanced and always on point. But when he speaks about the New Evangelization, you sense an additional enthusiasm. He is fired up about the subject, and you can hear his passion. From whence comes this enthusiasm?

The word "enthusiasm" is from the Greek, *en theos,* meaning "in God." Through the centuries, the word "enthusiasm" has been associated with various spiritual movements. If one was "enthusiastic," one was thought to be possessed by God and would speak in God's name. There is little doubt in my mind that the cardinal's enthusiasm comes from the Spirit, the same Spirit that is inspiring our popes to lead us in this New Evangelization.

But there is one ingredient for the New Evangelization that is missing, and without it, there will be no real possibility of success. What is missing are the priests. If you and I do not catch fire ourselves, if we do not promote the New Evangelization, it will surely not go anywhere. If we sit back and conduct business as usual, can there truly be a New Evangelization? Bishops are largely ineffectual without the support of their priests.

For me, the New Evangelization requires this catching fire, just as the cardinal is on fire. As the cardinal said, we need to have a sense of urgency. People all around us—family members, friends, neighbors, acquaintances, and people who work with us—have either lost the faith or never really had it to begin with. We do not need to go to the missions anymore to find people in need of hearing the Good News. They are sitting next to us.

Why the sense of urgency? One could ask, "What's the big deal?" But our faith is very clear. We read in the Acts of the Apostles: "There is no salvation through anyone else, nor is there any other name under heaven given to the human race by which we are to be saved" (Acts 4:12). To be a Christian requires that we believe Jesus Christ is the Way, the Truth, and the Life. He alone is the gate through which we pass to eternal life. Do you believe that? Sometimes priests stumble over this and say, "But what about those who are not Christians? Does this mean they cannot be saved?" We believe that many are saved who are not explicit Christians. Whom God chooses to save is reserved to him alone, but ultimately it is through Jesus Christ that anyone is saved. Our Christian faith tells us this for certain.

A sense of urgency should strike us. If that is true, then the New Evangelization is needed right now and the need around us is great. How many souls would be saved if only we priests and our people worked together to preach the Good News?

This type of evangelical approach is not typically part of our Catholic repertoire. For centuries, we have let people come to us. We do not feel comfortable going out and knocking on doors or preaching in the streets. We leave such things to the evangelical communities. They seem to be fearless about such things.

I think the Holy Spirit is calling us to "catch fire." I believe we are called to move out of our comfort zone and to become more "evangelical" ourselves. We ought to proclaim boldly the saving news of Jesus Christ. Acts 4, cited above, goes on to speak of the "boldness" of Peter and his preaching. We, too, ought to be bold in the Spirit.

In this, the young priests can help teach us. Among them, there is certainly a willingness to be more open and public about their faith. Instead of keeping it mostly private, as we older priests tend to do, the young are much more willing to proclaim their faith in the marketplace. Even wearing our clerics in public is a small beginning of our preaching to those who are no longer in the Christian community. Simply striking up a conversation on the faith with someone in the supermarket or on the street is another way to spread the Good News.

We cannot continue business as usual. The New Evangelization is not just one more program among many. It cannot simply die out next year, waiting for the next ecclesiastical endeavor. You and I need to change the way we do ministry. Instead of an introverted faith, we need an extroverted faith. We need to reach beyond those who come to our churches on Sunday. As Pope Francis said in his Chrism Mass homily to priests, "We need to 'go out,' then . . . to the 'outskirts' where there is suffering, bloodshed, blindness that longs for sight, and prisoners in thrall to many evil masters."[15]

We need the help of the people in the pews to make this New Evangelization happen. One person, that is, the priest, cannot convert a town. But an entire parish accompanied by their priest can certainly do so. Msgr. Jim O'Brien, a fine pastor from the Diocese of Syracuse, gave us a good example of how to begin the New Evangelization. Without a preconceived notion, he gathered a group of his parishioners at St. John's parish and they brainstormed. They decided to recruit laity in the parish as visitors. At Sunday masses, Msgr. O'Brien preached about this effort and eighty-two people signed up. The visitors were trained and then went out, two by two, to every dwelling within the parish boundaries. Those visited were informed of the faith community at St. John's. If they were members of other Christian congregations, they were supported in their religious faith. If they were fallen away Catholics or unchurched, they were encouraged to consider coming to St. John's. All those visited were invited to a parish picnic and to a session in the parish. Now, this is an ongoing program. Parishioners are assigned an area around their house, and they watch for newcomers who are then welcomed and given a copy of the parish brochure. In addition to reaching out to others, this program has made the people of St. John's a more welcoming community and more energized about sharing their faith.

As Cardinal Wuerl has been trying to get us to "catch fire" for the New Evangelization, we need to do so with our people. They need to hear our enthusiasm and to become enthusiastic themselves.

My brothers, the New Evangelization is dead in the water without us. I ask and implore each of you to open your hearts in prayer to the Lord and ask him to send down a Spirit of fire. May this Spirit fire each of us to not only become part of the evangelical work of the Church but also pass this Spirit on to the people whom we serve. United in the Spirit, you and your people will set your town ablaze!

I have come to set the earth on fire, and how I wish it were already blazing!

—Luke 12:49

A Fallen Brother

My Brothers,

Yesterday was not a good day. A classmate from the seminary was just arrested for selling drugs. Press accounts said he had gone on sabbatical last year after he was found to be cross-dressing and having sex in the rectory. It is said that he owned a sex shop. Now, federal authorities accused him of selling meth to undercover federal agents six times in the last five months.

I knew Kevin. He was a bright, energetic young seminarian. The news shocked me. As a priest-psychologist, I have been personally working with cases of priestly misconduct for twenty years. You would think I would not be shocked anymore. But I am. Perhaps it is because I knew Kevin and thought highly of him.

The last decade has brought cases of clerical sins and crimes to the front page of the paper. Just when we think it is safe to start reading the newspaper again, we are confronted with a brother involved in despicable behavior—the rector of the cathedral owning a sex shop and selling drugs?!

I must admit it makes me angry. Perhaps this is something we all, including the bishops, need to admit more publicly. Yes, the diocesan press release said we are praying for Kevin and we feel compassion. But we are also angry. How could he do such a thing? Jesus was angry at people in the Temple merely for exchanging money. He fashioned a "whip of cords" and violently threw them out (Jn 2:14–15). What would he say about this? We should be angry.

Kevin was well thought of in the diocese and was an aide to the bishop. He was the rector of the cathedral. He was known as a charismatic and gifted priest. The Holy Father made him a monsignor. All these things were true. How did such a terrific young man become a drug dealer and a peddler of deviant sexuality?

Psychology tends to be overly deterministic about human behavior. Psychological models look at people's genetics and biology plus their life experiences and upbringing and believe these account for people's behavior. It is somewhat true. A lot of who we are and how we act are strongly affected by our nature and our nurture. But people today often fall too easily into excusing their own behavior. They say, "I can't help it. It is because of what has happened to me that I am this way."

But this is not the whole picture. You and I are not completely determined by our biology and our experiences. We are not simply mechanical victims of all that we inherit. Our theology tells us of the importance of free will. You and I, made in the image of God, can choose. It is a powerful gift. It is a critical and integral part of what makes us human. Because we can choose, we participate in God's creation for ourselves and for our world. But we can also choose to participate in its destruction.

I do not know what happened to Kevin. More than likely, there were some childhood sexual conflicts and difficulties with which he came into adulthood. But there are many others who have similar conflicts who do not become drug dealers and purveyors of sexual deviancy. Kevin was responsible for finding healing in his own life and choosing the good. Somehow Kevin got involved in the darker side of humanity. Apparently, he did not seek help with his own "demons." One woman in a press account called his behavior "evil." It certainly was.

Drugs have become one of the great modern destroyers of humanity. It is surely an instrument of evil. In a bad moment, Kevin must have chosen to take his first dose of meth. All it takes is a "little" choice for evil to eventually unwrap our entire lives. Several people from Kevin's past said, "This man in the news is not the priest that I knew." Indeed, evil has concealed the face of the good man we knew, hopefully not forever.

My brothers, I wrote to you earlier about the little things and the little choices that we make. Little choices typically lead to big ones. I suspect if you showed Kevin, while he was in the seminary, his current "bio" in the newspaper, he would be shocked and frightened. He would likely be as dumbfounded as we are about how his life came to this.

We might be tempted to blame the diocesan vocation team or seminary. But we cannot blame everything on those responsible for his initial selection and formation. We cannot predict who a man will become thirty years later.

However, there are often early signs of issues that need to be addressed. My research suggests that there was a time in the seminary in the 1960s through the early 1980s when there was laxness in theological and psychological matters. We accepted a number of young men with sexual and other problems, and we were not rigorous enough in their screening and formation. While we have always had, and will always have, priests who end up having serious problems in ministry, my research suggests that there was a window of a couple of decades where we took in an unusually large number of unsuitable candidates. We are now paying a heavy price.

My brothers, I am sorry to bring Kevin's situation to your attention in this letter. But you are often faced with these media accounts. It is good for us to talk about it. We are hurting and angry because of these painful situations. I feel ashamed at such depravity in our midst. But I am also conscious of my own weakness and sinfulness. Surely we must all say, "There but for the grace of God go I."

I know that I still care about him and pray for his soul. I offered Mass this morning for my brother Kevin. He deserves to go to prison, and I understand he certainly will. He ought never serve as a priest in ministry again. He has forever lost this privilege.

Nevertheless, Kevin remains one of our brothers. We went to the seminary together. We concelebrated the Eucharist together. We gathered in priestly meetings together. We ministered side by side to the people of God. The same oils and hands that ordained us ordained him. I remember the bright, enthusiastic young man. I pray he becomes so again.

The Bishop, Our Brother

My Brothers,

I am concerned about the relationship between priests and bishops. I know many of you are concerned as well. The sex abuse crisis has precipitated some hard feelings toward bishops, although recently it has been abating. However, there may be an enduring fault line in this relationship if we do nothing. One bishop summarized the problem when he said to me, "A big mistake we made (in the crisis) was to use the phrase 'you priests.'"

There must always be some separation between priests and bishops. In any hierarchy, the boss is always a bit removed from the people he leads, although a good leader will work hard to stay connected and be a part of the team effort. Some leaders are more distant; others blend into the team and are barely distinguishable. But the tension between being part of a team and being its leader is always present.

The Vatican II document on bishops, *Christus Dominus*, gives us a summary of the relationship between bishops and priests: "Bishops should always embrace priests with a special love since the latter to the best of their ability assume the bishops' anxieties and carry them on day by day so zealously. They should regard the priests as sons and friends and be ready to listen to them" (16).

In its decree on priests, *Presbyterorum Ordinis*, the Council echoed similar ideas: "Therefore, on account of this communion in the same priesthood and ministry, bishops should regard priests as their brothers and friends" (7).

We see this same leadership tension in the Vatican documents. Priests are referred to as "brothers and friends" but also as "sons." The bishop is our shepherd and our leader. But he is also our brother.

I think some of us are worried that the balance is shifting too far away from being a brother. When a bishop said that their mistake was using the phrase "you priests," this statement implies that a bishop is not one of them. It implies that once a man is ordained a bishop, he stops becoming a priest: "You priests." This is theologically incorrect as well as a potential leadership disaster.

The social moat between priests and bishops these days is rather large. You see it especially in large gatherings of priests and bishops. There is little to no intermingling. Bishops have their own places to congregate, to vest, and to sit during the liturgy. Often they even eat by themselves. The impression given is that there is a caste society, and priests are part of the lower caste.

On the one hand, it is a mistake for bishops to eschew their role as leader and chief shepherd of the diocese. At the same time, it is equally a mistake to foster a caste society. One of the signs of a true Christian leader is that he leads as one who serves.

In my second parish, the pastor, Msgr. Peter Owens, was a holy man. While we shared duties during the Sacred Triduum, he insisted on being the one who washed the people's feet during the Holy Thursday liturgy. I must admit, I chafed a bit at this since I sometimes led the liturgy and wanted to perform this important part of the rite. But in retrospect I can understand his pastoral motives. It was an important symbol for the people of the parish to see their pastor humbly kneeling and washing their feet. For him it was not simply a once-a-year ritual—he served them throughout his many years with such humility.

In recent years, I have seen bishops trying to cross the "moat" and truly be brothers to their priests. Many bishops are now addressing their priests as "my brothers." This is important, and this nuance is not lost on the priests. They hear it, and they respond to it.

In the United Kingdom, there is a custom in some places of priests addressing their bishops with the simple title "Father." I heard it used again recently with the retired Cardinal of Westminster. It was said with respect, and it had an endearing quality to it. Whenever you hear it used, you sense a good bond between the priests and their bishop.

There are other ways I see bishops trying to cross the "moat." Many of them make a special effort to attend priest gatherings. In priest convocations, when the priests dress in casual clothes for a social occasion, bishops will often do the same. The bishops and their auxiliaries will sometimes separate themselves and sit with the priests at major dinners. Pope Francis himself, from the beginning of his pontificate, has given us many such gestures of brotherhood and humility. For example, he "crashed" the post-chrism Mass luncheon of seven priests of Rome who minister to the poor. To their delight, he shared in their informal, brotherly meal. Later, upon reflection, the priests were impressed that the pope really listened to them during the luncheon and they were touched by his relaxed, personal presence.[16] These "little" gestures on the part of bishops do not go unnoticed.

There is a natural tendency among us men to create rather stiff hierarchies, especially for those leaders who feel a bit insecure and feel a need to protect themselves and their role. As they grow more comfortable in their leadership positions, they relax a bit and lead more naturally. I found this to be so for myself as the CEO of Saint Luke Institute for over a dozen years. The Christian community calls for all of us to be brothers and sisters, while recognizing the bishop as first among the brothers and our chief shepherd. We are not so much a rigid hierarchy as a community of disciples, each with different gifts and each with different vocations within the community.

We priests have an important role to play in the relationship between bishops and priests. We tend to put the onus completely on the bishop and blame him if the relationship goes sour. But a relationship is a two-way street. If he is also our brother, then we should not forget to give him all the love and support that a brother deserves.

If the relationship between the priests and their bishop is not ideal, priests should also work directly to ameliorate it. For example, I know of a diocese that had a strained relationship between the bishop and his priests. The priests politely and discreetly raised the issue with him, and both have been working to make it better. The healing began with the bishop holding a listening session just with his priests. Significant progress has already being made. Priests typically respond very positively to such a humble gesture.

My own bishop is a good man of faith, and he works hard. He tries to listen to his priests and to the laity, and to support them. He is good about sending us little notes to congratulate us and to acknowledge our ministry. I try to return the favor. I suspect bishops appreciate our gratitude more than we realize. Have you ever sent your bishop a letter of support? Do you compliment him when he does something well? We priests hope and expect he will do so for us. We ought to do the same for him.

I personally believe that we have today the holiest group of popes, bishops, and priests in the entire history of the Church. Does this sound a bit too cheerily optimistic? Read your church history and then look, for example, at the popes we have had in recent times: John XXIII, Paul VI, John Paul I, John Paul II, Benedict XVI, and now Francis whose humble gestures have captivated the world, much like his namesake.

I had the honor of meeting Benedict XVI once. He was a cardinal at the time and his soft-spoken humility made a strong impression. Benedict's elected retirement reminds me of his humility and his desire only to serve—and when that was no longer possible, he willingly stepped down from a position of great power. How many world leaders would do the same? Each pope in recent time has been different and has had different gifts, but each has been a devoted man of God. I say the same for the bishops and priests we have today. I am proud to be one of you.

I do not want to overemphasize the problem between bishops and priests today. My research found that the strong majority of priests like their bishops and report having a good relationship with them. The data indicate that over three-quarters of priests say their relationship with their bishop is good.[17] Compared to how most Americans look at their secular bosses, this is astoundingly high. But the relationship between priest and bishop is critical for the life of the priest and the entire presbyterate, as well as for the bishop. Priests and bishops ought to work regularly to make this critical bond a strong one.

A while back I was visiting Archbishop Wilton Gregory. I have always admired him as one of our finest bishops and leaders. We were sharing a quiet moment in his residence, and he was reminiscing about how much he enjoyed being with the people of his archdiocese and with the priests. He spoke fondly of his priests and said from the heart, "I can truly say that I love them." It was a touching moment. The next day, I stood in front of the priests to give them a day of recollection. At one point, I happened to mention that they were fortunate to have such a good bishop.

The priests spontaneously broke into loud applause. Their bishop loved them, and they knew it.

When the relationship among priests is strong and they truly are brothers, and when bishops and priests are likewise truly brothers in the Lord, we are closer to what Jesus calls us to be. This unity is integral to our effectiveness and our happiness, and the people of God benefit greatly. Such a harmonious unity will likewise be an important spur to vocations; more young men will want to join our company.

I would like to be so bold as to end with a word from us priests to our bishops.

Dear Bishop, we thank you for tirelessly working for the sanctity of all the people and for us priests. We know that you have great hopes for us and that you work tirelessly to serve us. We thank you for allowing us to share in your great work. It is our honor to help shoulder a little bit of the burden. We recognize you as a successor to the Apostles, and we know you also as our brother. Remember that you can always count on us for support, for prayers, and to be a friend, especially when times are hard. We are brothers. We know that you love us. We thank you and we love you.

Preaching the Bad News

My Brothers,

We have all had those "ah hah" moments during our priesthood when something struck us and it changed the way we thought about our lives and ministries. One such moment for me occurred in the seminary. It was a preaching class taught by Father Gabriel O'Donnell, O.P., and it is a story I often tell. At one point Father Gabriel looked at us and said, "It is easier to preach the bad news than it is the good news." It hit me strongly then and has continued to be a part of my thinking about priesthood.

It is very easy to preach the bad news. In fact, in the first few years of priesthood and of writing homilies, I found his admonition to be quite true. My first reflections on the gospel passage often fell into the category of bad news. If I took my first response to the gospel and preached about it, it would come out as a negative homily that made people feel chastened. Of course, such homilies need to be given from time to time, for example during Lent.

However, Father O'Donnell encouraged us to see the good news in the scripture passages on which we were preaching. We ask ourselves, "What is the good news that Jesus is offering today to the people of God?" This is a more challenging homily to write. It is easy to make people feel bad. But how can we inspire people to the good, helping them to see the beauty of our God and their own beauty? Will people walk out of church today with their heads up or their heads down? The latter is easier, the former more difficult.

This has become especially important for our day. Secular society paints religion and especially Catholicism as a negative, life-denying institution that is an unwanted remnant from ancient superstitions. Sadly, at times, we have fed into this stereotype. The dour priest always condemning people from the pulpit unwittingly feeds this caricature.

Coming back from the synod on the New Evangelization, Cardinal Wuerl told us of a Nigerian woman who gave an excellent intervention during the synod. At one point during her talk she stopped, looked around, and said, "You know you can smile! Priests are allowed to smile. And that goes for bishops too!" It is hard to preach a message of joy with a glum look on one's face. The best vocational poster is a happy priest.

One such happy bishop is Cardinal Dolan. His energy, enthusiasm, and beaming optimism are infectious. During a media interview after being named the Archbishop of New York, he was asked if there was anything he would like to condemn. He said, "Yes, I condemn instant mashed potatoes and light beer."[18] It was a masterful response. The reporter would have painted Cardinal Dolan with the same negative, condemning Church brush. The quick-witted cardinal not only did not fall into the trap but also reversed the stereotype with a rather funny retort. And anyone who knows the cardinal knows that the man likes his beer full and his potatoes real.

This was not a lucky, chance response by the cardinal. For all his quick-witted retorts, he is a serious thinker and an intelligent man. He is well aware of the secular negative stereotype, and he actively fights against it. Later in a *New York Times* interview, he revealed it explicitly: "What weighs on me the most is the caricature of the Catholic Church as crabby, nay-saying, down in the dumps, discouraging, on the run. And I'm thinking if there is anything that should be upbeat, affirming, positive, joyful, it should be people of faith."[19] I thank God for Cardinal Dolan and think God picked him as the right man to lead the Church in our time.

He reminds me of another churchman also with a ready smile and humorous story—Pope John XXIII. Each year in my course on pastoral theology, I insist the seminarians read his opening speech to the Second Vatican Council. Here, from the sovereign pontiff, we find similar words:

> In the daily exercise of our pastoral office, we sometimes have to listen, much to our regret, to voices of persons who, though burning with zeal, are not endowed with too much sense of discretion or measure. In these modern times they can see nothing

but prevarication and ruin. They say that our era, in comparison with past eras, is getting worse, and they behave as though they had learned nothing from history, which is, none the less, the teacher of life. . . . We feel we must disagree with those prophets of gloom.

There is something intrinsically Christian to be people of hope and true optimism. How can we not be people who smile and are joyful when we have been given the gift of life here and now, and the promise of eternal life in Jesus? If we truly understood what is ours as adopted sons and daughters of God, we would be radiant with happiness. Should at least a little of this salvation seep into our faces and our lives? As the woman told the bishops at the New Evangelization synod, "You know you can smile!"

Some people, even some of our brothers, have equated orthodoxy with dourness and a pervasive negativism. In our day, as in good Pope John XXIII's day, there are prophets of gloom who though burning with zeal also lack of a sense of discretion and of history. These dour prophets can manipulate groups of priests and attempt to wield influence in our Church. But their depressive judgmentalism only fans the flames of secularism and its religious caricature.

While we Christians are certainly critical toward the creeping secular atheism of our time, this is overshadowed by our surpassing joy of knowing Jesus Christ. In fact, I would go so far as to say that dourness and negativism are a counterwitness to the Gospel. Who can believe in the words coming from such a face? The following words of scripture should hold a central place in our hearts: "Rejoice in the Lord always. I shall say it again: rejoice! Your kindness should be known to all" (Phil 4:4–5).

My brothers, let us begin to preach the Good News with our lives, our faces, and our demeanors. As Pope Francis said, "A good priest can be recognized by the way his people are anointed: this is a clear proof. When our people are anointed with the oil of gladness, it is obvious: for example, when they leave Mass looking as if they have heard good news."[20]

Do not let yourselves be manipulated by media stereotypes or by a few dour brothers who try to make us into unhappy replicas of themselves. We priests are Christians, we are brothers, and we are people who have inherited everything from an infinitely generous God. Thus, we are filled with joy. This joy is our best homily. This joy is also a true sign that the salvation of Christ is upon us.

For the kingdom of God is not a matter of food and drink, but of righteousness, peace and joy in the Holy Spirit.

—Romans 14:17

Grateful, Eucharistic Hearts

My Brothers,

I would like you to have a grateful heart. To be a Christian and to be a priest especially requires a grateful heart. Christians are those who give thanks. We priests lead them in the greatest act of thanksgiving, the Eucharist. Indeed, this prayer of thanksgiving, done in Jesus' name and with one configured to him presiding, makes Jesus' saving act present again. Precisely in this act of thanksgiving our salvation is once again made real.

One must say then that the priest ought to be a model of gratitude—he stands in front of the assembled people of God and voices the community's thanksgiving. There is something incongruous about a sour priest with a negative attitude. As Pope Francis exhorted his brothers in his first address to the College of Cardinals, "Let us never yield to pessimism, to that bitterness that the devil offers us every day."[21]

Rather, the priest's face and his demeanor ought to speak of his own gratitude and thanksgiving. It is

difficult for anyone to claim to be a Christian and not
be, fundamentally, a grateful person. Christianity without gratitude is unthinkable. Priests are to be examples
and teachers of gratitude.

Yet I think it is more difficult in our day to be
a people of gratitude. The narcissism all around us
breeds an entitlement culture. Narcissists unrealistically
believe that they deserve to be treated better than others and are offended, perhaps even angry, when they
are not given their due. Therefore, narcissists are never
really grateful. They never really believe they receive
their due. To be grateful is certainly countercultural in
many places today.

Growing up, my parents never heard the word
"narcissism." They grew up in an immigrant culture.
My mom was born in Norway, and my dad's folks
came from Italy. They both grew up in neighboring
towns near Boston, and they were poor. In addition to
having little education and training, it was the Great
Depression and everyone they knew was poor. My dad
told us of times when there was not enough to eat.

Their goal was to make a life for their families, to
do better. They knew they would have to work hard
and sacrifice. But, as my dad told us, "The idea was
that your children would have a better life." They
worked and sacrificed for us. They lived simply, for-
going expensive vacations and other luxuries, even
when there was finally some money, so that we could
live a secure life. In their youth, neither of them or
their families ever went to college. But we children
all went to college—they made sure of that. When we
graduated, they were very proud. Ultimately, all of

us received graduate degrees. Our parents loved and
sacrificed for their children. They even gave us "seed"
money to begin our adult lives, something they never
had. Now, in their old age, they have the satisfaction
and fulfillment of having prosperous adult children.

We, their children, are grateful for the sacrifice and
love of our parents. We can readily see what was done
for us. We recognize that it was not our right to have
all these benefits. We learned it was the result of the
hard work and sacrifice on the part of loving parents.

Such things teach us about the faith. We learn
what true love is: It means sacrificing for the other.
We learn to be grateful because of what was given to
us by parents who loved and sacrificed. These values
encapsulate much of Christianity. It is a short trip from
family values to Christian values. Thus the family is
truly the domestic church that teaches us about our
loving, self-sacrificing God whom we call Father.

I am not sure how to teach people today about
Christianity. This afternoon I have a class with the
seminarians on redemption and salvation. These soon-
to-be priests will be challenged to make these concepts
come alive and be real for the people of today. Humankind has been saved by the loving self-sacrifice of God.
The hearts of all people should be full of gratitude. But
the first response of many people to the Good News
of redemption is, "What sin? I haven't done anything
wrong."

People today want to get what they believe is rightfully theirs. As the television commercials suggest, "I
want it all and I want it now." And when they do
not get their "rights," they are visibly angry. They

feel like victims. Someone or something has violated their rights. They want what they deserve. They want justice!

In the Christian dispensation, we do not deserve salvation. We do not deserve the wonderful divine gifts that God showers on us. They are freely given. Without God's gift, we would be lost. But it is God's desire that not one of us would be lost, and the gift of salvation is offered to all who would accept it. It takes humility to allow God to love us so completely.

Narcissism is a burden. I have worked with many narcissists in psychotherapy, and narcissism is no fun for them. It is a ponderous life full of imagined hurts and disappointments. They are angry and do not understand why people will not give them what they "deserve." Underneath it all, they are not at peace. There is a constant tug of war between their hidden poor self-image and their surface bravado and arrogance.

Frankly, I am not sure how to teach the people of today this sense of gratitude. Maybe we cannot. Perhaps it is something not taught but rather caught. Maybe we should not so much talk to them about it but lead them into an experience of it.

Perhaps it begins by tasting, for just a moment, the beauty and generosity of our God. Just as children may experience the loving sacrifice of their parents, so might we experience the loving sacrifice of our heavenly Father. When we are filled, if only for a brief moment, with the overwhelming holiness and love of God, the false idols that cloud our minds dissipate. For a moment, we can see the truth. Such beauty! Such wondrous love! Such infinite kindness!

When we see such infinite holiness, the muck of our lives and our world becomes painfully apparent. It was Peter, upon seeing the miraculous catch of fish and being overwhelmed by grace, who thus saw his own brokenness: "Depart from me Lord, for I am a sinful man" (Lk 5:8). When we see the blazing and pure glory of God, we recognize we are not so wonderful as we thought. The world, too, is mired in imperfection and sin. Clearly the infinitely loving God we just tasted did not do this. There must be another source of the brokenness and darkness.

You, my brothers, give them a taste of this loving God. You give them a taste of the One who sacrificed himself in love for them. The Eucharist is not only a time when we give thanks in that most perfect way, but it is also a school that teaches us to give thanks. Sacraments make present what they signify. The Eucharist signifies our thanksgiving; it also teaches us to be grateful.

You and I are men of the Eucharist. "There can be no Eucharist without the priesthood, just as there can be no priesthood without the Eucharist."[22] Because of our great Catholic sacramental theology and life, we recognize that the "stuff" of this world, when transformed by Christ, becomes the instrument of our salvation. In the Eucharist, we taste and take in the life of our God.

What a great gift it is! Each day this reality is re-presented. And from time to time, God gives us the grace consciously to experience the consolation of tasting the Lord's goodness. "Taste and see that the Lord is good" (Ps 34:9). Is there any wonder we priests never tire of presiding at the Eucharist? It could seem like such a rote daily ritual. How could it carry such significance? But more and more it becomes the center of our lives.

Thus, we become grateful people. The next time we step up to the altar, having celebrated the Mass the day before, our hearts are a bit more grateful and the words of thanksgiving that we pray become a bit more meaningful. We are increasingly absorbed into the mysterious action that takes place. We offer our little personal sufferings on the altar, mixed with those of the Son. We too, for just a moment, are taken up into the saving mystery.

If there will be anything to break the narcissism of today, it must be the Eucharist. There we taste a self-sacrificing love, a love that every true parent instinctively understands. There, we recipients are the grateful sons and daughters of a loving Father who has sacrificed himself completely for us. In this eternal moment, we recognize that we have been given an inestimable gift, not deserved but gratefully received.

Our lives ultimately become one Eucharistic act. We are those whose whole lives must become an act of thanksgiving. Filled with God, reflecting a unity with the Son, we live in one continuous, graced moment. Such gratitude eventually beams from our faces breaking into a broad smile and with eyes dancing with light. I have seen more than a few older priests whose faces glow with such grace.

When the last day comes and the new age dawns, it will be a gentle transition to eternity. Our praise and thanksgiving will join in the chorus of countless voices of gratitude. We are the grateful sons and daughters of an infinitely loving God. At the altar, we tasted it. In life, we tried to live it. Now, it is ours forever.

Rejoice always. Pray without ceasing. In all circumstances give thanks, for this is the will of God for you in Christ Jesus.

—1 Thessalonians 5:16–17

A Note to My Younger Brothers

My Brothers,

My younger brothers, I did not want to let this opportunity pass without offering a word of thanksgiving and encouragement to you. Whenever our presbyterate gathers, I see a group of younger priests, and it gives me great encouragement. I thank you for responding to God's call. The work of Jesus will continue. There will be hands to harvest the fields. But, especially, it is who you are that is a source of hope for me.

I have worked in the formation of priests for a number of years. These last few years, I have been working daily in seminary formation. I can honestly say that I think you, our younger priests, will be better than we were. My brothers and I responded as best we could. We all had our moments of greatness, and our failings, as will you. But your zeal, your commitment, and the strength of your cohort suggest to me a new "army" for Christ. God has picked you to be the army for the New Evangelization. You are well suited to the task.

If you will please indulge me, I would like to offer a few reflections. I hope you find something helpful herein.

My first thought is that priesthood is worth it. If there is anything we can give you, we older priests, it is the assurance that priesthood is indeed worth the sacrifice. It is worth it not only for the people but also for you personally. As in any life, there will be temptations and trials. Should you find yourself suffering anything, please know that marriage or any other life will unlikely fix the very human challenges of boredom, conflict, loneliness, tiredness, and a host of other human experiences that come with living. These must be endured. But as priests, we endure them in faith. They are passing.

Once you have been ordained, don't look back. Keep your eyes fixed on the prize, as St. Paul tells us. Press ahead. The best is indeed yet to come. I can honestly say that each year in priesthood I have felt stronger, more at home, and more at peace. So will you. But it is a life of trust. We priests are not exempt from the need to grow in trust and in faith. Despite all of our theological education and our "inside track" into the things of God, at root we too are people of faith. We, too, must grow in a loving trust of our Father. Our journey, like that of the people, is a journey of faith. "At present we see indistinctly, as in a mirror, but then face to face" (1 Cor 13:12).

The witness and example of our elderly priests is, for us, an assurance and a guidepost. When we see their lovely faces full of peace and radiating joy, we have a living witness of God's faithfulness to his priests. He did not abandon his Son Jesus. He will not abandon us.

My second thought is never stop praying. As the years have passed, I have increasingly realized that it is indeed God who daily supports me. The "amount" of grace I need each day to be a priest seems to be actually increasing down through the years. I can sometimes feel God pouring his strength into me when I pray. I walk out of the chapel reenergized, balanced, and rooted. God is upholding me. For you, this cannot be some kind of abstract theological concept; it must be a living reality in your life.

There are too many forces, human and preternatural, that would push you off center and eventually lead you in the wrong direction. It happens subtly and little bits at a time. The Holy Spirit will guide you. It is impossible for us to discern by ourselves what is truly right. We need this Spirit for our own sake and for the sake of our people. May God give us a taste for all that is good and an ability to discern what is evil. I pray this for you and for myself.

I am happy to say that your generation seems to know this already. You are more dedicated to prayer from the beginning than we were. I see many of you doing daily holy hours, reflecting upon scripture, faithfully reciting the Liturgy of the Hours, saying the Rosary, and engaged in regular mental prayer. These will serve you well.

I am grateful for your faithfulness to our tradition. You love our Catholic faith, and you love our Holy Father. You are faithful to its teachings, and you enthusiastically pass them on to the people of God. This is another blessing you bring to the priesthood and to the Church.

But remember to be obedient to your bishop. What you have in enthusiasm and in zeal must be tempered with discernment and the Spirit. It is your bishop who has been given the grace of leadership of the diocese. He is the visible sign of the Church, whom you love. You may agree with him or not on some issues, but regardless, follow him. You will not be lost when following this successor of the apostles.

Similarly, listen to the older priests. There is a collection of wisdom and experience among them. In my early years of priesthood, I had many pastoral ideas. Some were terrific. Some were a little off. The older priests were helpful guides for me. They kept me from doing some dumb things pastorally. Listen to them. You need them just as they need you.

Follow your passion. We are all priests. However, each of us has different gifts. Some of you are good liturgists and have a charism for it. Develop that gift. Learn what you can and promote good liturgy. Some may like to study canon law (not my gift!). God knows we need canon lawyers. Some of you love spirituality. There are lots of opportunities to learn more about our Catholic spirituality and to teach it at the diocesan level and in the parish.

The diocese and the parish needs your gifts, and you need to develop them. A passion squelched only leads to discouragement and dissatisfaction. When you follow your passion, you become even more excited and enthusiastic about the priesthood. You also become a greater resource for the local people and the wider Church.

Please, for the sake of the people, improve your homilies. This is one of the greatest complaints of the people in the pews. Our homilies are not good enough. Sometimes, they are boring. Often, they answer questions people are not asking. The homily is the vehicle by which you will reach more people than any other.

Not all of you will be great homilists, but we can all be better. If you start working on your Sunday homilies as early as Monday, and perhaps use a team of the laity to assist you, you will find your homilies getting better. Don't be afraid to ask for help and to get more training in homiletics. I used to have the permanent deacon in my parish listen to a draft of my homily during the week and help me with it. When Sunday comes, it is a wonderful boost to our priesthood when people say, "Nice homily Father!" It is a source of much priestly satisfaction to be a good preacher.

One of the most important things I can pass along is the need to err on the side of mercy. I remember Msgr. Joe Champlin, a holy priest from my diocese, noted author, and fine pastor, once told me that he only denied absolution in the confessional one time in forty years and that was a mistake. While we do not compromise the integrity of our Catholic teaching, priests are regularly called upon to make pastoral judgments. Whenever you have such a judgment to make, I recommend that, if in doubt, err on the side of mercy. The mercies of our God are endlessly poured out to us each day. The Church, if it is anything, must be merciful.

There are a few of my thoughts. After years in the priesthood, you yourselves will become mentors for the younger men. Love them as God does. He picked them. They will not be perfect, but they will be just the right priests for their new times. The Spirit will inspire you with what to say to them, just as I hope the Spirit has inspired me to hear correctly.

Thank you, my younger brothers. As the years have passed, my arms have grown a little weary. But when I see your faces, I am buoyed up with new strength and encouragement. Thank you for listening to me. Thank you for being coworkers in the Lord's vineyard. I am proud to say we are brothers. You and I are priests together.

"It will come to pass in the last days," God says, "that I will pour out a portion of my spirit upon all flesh. Your sons and daughters shall prophesy, your young men shall see visions, your old men shall dream dreams."

—Acts 2:17

Dream Big

Dear Brothers,

People's dreams are too small. The narcissist wants the applause of the public and the adoration of others. The materialist wants a big house and a large bank account. I know a number of people with one or both of these; some are happy and content, and others are not. Their happiness depends little on these things, and very often, possessions and applause are actually a burden. Ironically, the dreams of narcissists and materialists are much too small.

You cannot really be a Christian without big dreams. We need to imagine a lot. Imagine a God who is infinite and reaches down to us finite humans. Imagine an uncreated Being offering creatures a full share in infinity. Imagine beyond the veil of this life an existence that stretches our minds beyond what can be comprehended. Imagine the deity as a loving Father and we as true sons and daughters. This is the incredulous stuff of fairy tales. Only a madman (or a Christian) would believe it!

I remember a brother priest who told me about a pastoral visit he made. He visited an elderly lady who was very sick. She apparently was not practicing any faith. He spoke to her about Jesus and the Father. He told her about the forgiveness of sins and the promise of eternal life with God. He told her about heaven. When he finished giving witness, she promptly said, "I don't believe in such fairy tales!" The next day, she died.

When you stop to think about it, she had something true to say. The promises of our God and what Jesus has done for us are so fantastic they strain credibility. As they say, "It is too good to be true. What's the catch?" To complete the unbelievable nature of this whole story, there is no catch. It is all God's free gift to us.

If there is any struggle to believing in God and having faith in the Christian message, it ought to be that it seems too wonderful to be true. To be a Christian, you have to be able to dream very big.

I was in a beautiful park in South Africa one afternoon with a young priest and a lay woman. They had just come from the funeral of a friend. She had stopped practicing her Catholic faith some time ago. We were sitting on a bench in Groot Constantia. This is a beautiful wine estate with acres and acres of vineyards nestled against Table Mountain. The air was fresh, and the sun was out. The woman sighed wistfully, thinking about her deceased friend, and said, "I hope that heaven is as nice as this."

I thought the comment was one of the saddest things I had ever heard. Is that the best she can imagine? Is that what she is hoping for—that heaven be like a beautiful park? I truly believe that many, many people do not believe in heaven or, if they do, they have a conception similar to the one this woman had. For them, heaven is a nice park.

Some of the more "spiritually minded" folks in our secular age tell me they think of the next life as a kind of reabsorption into the cosmos. They say we become one with all of creation in a kind of pantheistic union. In recent years, I have heard it quite a bit. I presume this means we lose our consciousness as a person. But why would I as a person want to be united with a rock? Sounds like hell to me.

As our secular culture is losing a sense of God, it is, of course, losing a sense of heaven. There should be no wonder that our dreams have shrunk and we have become trapped in our own material world and its narrow thinking. All that is left is a pessimism that masquerades as "realism" and a pitiful hope in a world that continually disappoints. Our dreams are becoming much too small.

The Christian understanding of heaven is to be one with our infinite, loving God. We enter a loving union more intimate than we have ever known. God's being "courses" through our being. We do not lose our humanity and consciousness. Love unites without destroying or subjugating. It fulfills the other while not losing anything of itself. We actually become more ourselves and more alive in love. This is the nature of real love.

And another astounding teaching of our faith is that this heaven, this union with God, is not just reserved for the next life. No, in the person of Jesus, God with us, the kingdom is already breaking into our world. Right now, we begin to taste this union with God.

This is yet another wonderful reality of our Christian faith that is unmatched throughout history. God now dwells in us. "Whoever loves me will keep my word, and my Father will love him, and we will come to him and make our dwelling with him" (Jn 14:23). Once again, we priests know that it is precisely in the Eucharist where this union reaches its apex in this life. We literally ingest the God-man and become one with him.

You and I can sympathize with those who do not believe. Even in Jesus' day, it was difficult to believe. After Jesus spoke to them, "Whoever eats my flesh and drinks my blood remains in me and I in him" (Jn 6:56), some of his disciples left. They murmured, "This saying is hard; who can accept it?" (Jn 6:60).

Becoming one with the divinity is something that strains our ability to comprehend. Yet, Jesus prayed for it, and he promised it. In his priestly prayer at the Last Supper, Jesus prayed to the Father, "that the love with which you loved me may be in them and I in them" (Jn 17:26). He also said, "As you, Father, are in me and I in you, that they also may be in us" (Jn 17:21).

Jesus did not shy away from telling this immense truth . . . nor should we. We priests need to help our people dream big. Forget the nice parks. Forget the applause of others and the big houses. What God offers is infinitely more. He offers himself to us, completely.

He will dwell in us, and we will become one. The Eucharist is a foretaste and the seed of that immense gift.

We can only begin to understand this when we understand what love is. As our world has lost its God, it is descending into narcissism and violence. As it loses God, it loses love. What it ends up with is shattered hopes, a distorted sexuality, and widespread addiction. Only God can give us the love that suffices.

Christianity is a religion with a big dream. It is a dream that became a reality in Jesus. In his Church, this reality comes to us now, this day. I can understand the woman who thought it was a fairy tale—Christianity is a fairy tale beyond all others. I am sad, however, that she could not embrace it. Deep in our hearts is an inchoate sense that it is true. Somehow we realize that, beyond all imagining, it is true. This is the seed of faith.

My brothers, let us dream big. We need to teach the people to dream big. In the Eucharist, we offer them a taste of that dream come true.

Brothers Forever

Dear Brothers,

Sometimes I wonder about the next life; I do not know that I will be saved. As the years pass, I think we all become more acutely aware of our sins and weaknesses. And we become aware of how seemingly intractable they are. After all these years of priesthood, why are we not any better? We can only rely on God's mercy. We must do so.

It makes me a bit sad to think I might not be among the elect. But who am I to stand among the likes of John Vianney, Mother Teresa, John of the Cross, John Paul II, Teresa of Avila, and the host of martyrs? I was hoping to spend the next life praising God and thanking him for his wonderful generosity. It would be a great sadness to lose this. In the eternal darkness, there is no thought of praising God.

Then, two thoughts come to me. First, I must entrust everything to God in this life and in the next. So, I must entrust my eternal disposition to him. I trust that God will do what is right. I am responsible for living as best I can now; I leave the future to him. Second, if I cannot praise him in the next life, then I vow to do so to my utmost in this life. If I cannot praise and thank him in the next, I will do so now. Let us then not waste one moment. Let no instant pass by when we do not give God thanks and praise.

This fills me with joy. What a grace and opportunity we have been given to praise and thank God in this life. It is a blessing for us to do so. Is that really not our first call as Christians and especially as priests? Of course, we work hard in the Lord's vineyard to preach the Good News. We are dedicated to the New Evangelization. We want everyone to hear about Jesus.

But our first call as people of God is to thank and praise him. For what do we praise and thank God? Of course, he has done so many wonderful things for us. A lifetime would not be enough to recount them all and to give sufficient thanks. But most of all, we thank God just for being God. We thank him for just being himself.

Isn't it wonderful to look into the face of God and marvel at such love, such beauty, such joy! What a gift it is to see the face of God in our hearts! I must confess, when I look upon his face, I am filled with joy and thanksgiving. "Father, I thank you. In this moment, I do not thank you for anything you have done. No. I am thanking you for just being. I love to look upon your face. I thank you for just being you."

This, my brothers, is our primary call. As men of God, our first calling is to be a people who look upon God's face and give thanks. This is our first vocation and our joy. Of course, this spontaneous love and thanksgiving for God is itself a grace. God himself grants us the grace to gaze upon his face in our prayer. He allows us to look upon him with only the thinnest veil of separation. One day we hope and pray he will "tear through the veil of this sweet encounter."[23]

What is the work that our brothers and sisters in heaven do? Their only work is to praise God, and it is enough. We do not know if we will join their blessed company in the future, so let us join it now. Let us learn to love God more and to praise God more in this life.

How blessed we are to be ministers of the Eucharist. It is our central prayer and it is our lifeblood because praising God is our central work and it is our life. It is precisely when we stand at the altar that we join the timeless host of heaven. Here we are privileged to be one with them, thanking and praising the God of us all. This is why we are priests.

Why do we get so caught up in the affairs of this world? They are swiftly passing. We become so concerned about projects and programs, as if the fate of the kingdom rested on us. We witness easily to the burden of time; may we also witness to the freedom of eternity. And one drop of divine grace surpasses our multitudinous human works.

Our thoughts and our focus might be how we can better thank and praise God today. We do not know if we will be given such a blessed chance tomorrow. So we start by gazing into the face of our beautiful God today. In such a gaze, we are filled with eternity. For a moment, all of our burdens melt away, thus "leaving

my cares forgotten among the lilies."[24] These are the
sublime tastes of the next life that God gives us. Can
anyone doubt the reality and future offer of heaven?
Even now, heaven is breaking into our world.

I would like to spend today learning to love God
more. Of myself, I do not know how to accomplish
this. I could search and fill my head with sacred ideas,
as we theologians are wont to do, but it wouldn't
work. These ideas cannot cross the gulf between time
and eternity. I know that only God can reach across
and give this grace. He alone can allow us to gaze upon
his face and to rejoice in him.

At times, the dry days come. For some, they last for
decades. I marvel at the strength of Mother Teresa's
faith. In a collection of Mother's letters to her spiritual
director, she revealed her painful years of dryness, when
she could no longer look upon God's face in prayer.
She wrote, "As for me, the silence and the emptiness
is so great, that I look and do not see,—Listen and do
not hear."[25] But she pressed on with her ministry and
with her prayer.

These are the great souls and the great saints. You
and I could not stand so much trial, so much emptiness. They enter the kingdom in triumph; we hope in
God's mercy. I remember the priest, mentioned earlier,
who said he was saved from the eternal darkness by the
intercession of Mary with her Son. I pray for her to
remember me on the last day.

It is good to let go of concern for the next life
and simply commend it to God. For now, we have
a chance to thank God and to praise him. I realize
that the Mass I celebrated this morning could have

been more reverent, more focused on him and less on myself. I ought to have prayed more before it and during it. I resolve to try to do better. I will try to make tomorrow's Mass more of a complete self-offering so that I might be totally on the paten, as Jesus is completely there as well.

As I go about my day, obsessed with so many mundane things, I reserve a "corner" of my heart and my mind for him. He is never outside of my thoughts. As the years have passed, he gives us the grace of walking perpetually with him. It typically brings a little smile to my face and my heart senses his perpetual loving presence. My smile and my heart continually praise and thank him. There is indeed only a thin "veil" between us. It can be easily rent, and sometime soon, it will be.

I will be sad to let go of my friends in this world. My brothers, I will miss you. But there are many, many priests waiting for us. I would like to be able to thank those priests, face-to-face, who have been so generous to me. They will be there. God rewards them for their generosity.

We rely on their prayers as well. Their priestly ministry has not ended. They remember those of us who still labor on this earth. They know how hard we try, and they know of our faithful labors. Those priests above must be powerful intercessors for us priests below.

Could it be that some of the graces we priests receive now come through the hands of our brothers in heaven? Has their priestly intercessory role ended? I think not. If Thérèse of Lisieux could say, "I will spend my heaven doing good on earth," perhaps we can as well. This we hope for.

My brothers, I do not know the future. But if God grants me the chance, I will offer it for you. I believe many of our brothers who have gone before us have already done so. No doubt, you will do the same.

We never stop being priests. We never stop raising our hands in prayer. We never stop giving thanks and praising God. We never stop standing in the breech, interceding for others. We never stop being brothers.

One Final Note

Dear Brothers,

As I look over these letters, I realize that I wanted to do more. I wanted to reach out of the pages and to embrace each of you. I wanted to transmit the love God has for you and the love that I have for you.

I wanted to remind you of the beautiful Mother that we have. I believe that it was she who chose me to be a priest. Perhaps it was the same for you? You already are her devoted sons.

I wanted to warn you about the mistakes some of our brothers have made. I have seen the deep devastation in the wake of such sins. It pains me to see it. I do not want to see you, and the people, suffer so.

I wanted all of us to learn to love the Church even more. It is a living, dynamic fount of grace. Filled with imperfect people like us, it is nevertheless a beautiful gift.

With you, I wanted to work together to heal the divisions in our priesthood. They hurt the Church, and they hurt us. When we speak ill of a brother, it is not our Father's work that we do.

Most of all, I deeply desire that you and I love God more. Today, we can praise God more. Today, we can thank him more. This is a wonderful privilege. Let us not waste even a moment.

Forgive me for not being able to pass on to you all that I had hoped. I know that God will make up for my lack. I know that you already are filled with such graces and more.

I would like to end as I began, with gratitude. Please know that I am filled with gratitude for you. How much more must God be filled with such gratitude? You do his work with dedication and faith, at no small cost to yourself. God is never outdone in generosity.

Even now, you and I receive back one hundredfold. We are filled with a sense of peace in Jesus' presence. We have a sense of fulfillment that our lives make an eternal difference for many. How great must be the joy of a priest in the next life to greet a brother or sister whom he has helped to find salvation.

I thank you for all you have done for others. I thank you for what you have done, and will do, for me. I am confident that in my last hours, one of you will minister to me. One of you, my brothers, will anoint me. You will hear my last confession. You will give me the Body and Blood of Jesus. You will be with me at the end.

During the Mass, you and my bishop will gather around the altar and pray. As my casket is carried out, you will be my pallbearers. You will chant the Salve Regina, which I love so. You will carry me to the cemetery and lay me next to my brothers. I know that you will remember me in your Masses for our deceased priests. I thank you.

I, for my part, promise to remember you. If God gives me the grace, I will pray for you. I will stand with all the brothers and ask that you receive a double portion of the Spirit. We will long for the day when you will join us. Just a little longer, and the sun will rise.

Then, you and I will turn our heads together and face the living God. The radiance of his love and his joy will fill us completely. Then, my brothers . . . together . . . we will shine forever in the light.

Postscript

Looking toward the future, society's forecast is not good. I would like to be able to say that conditions are going to get better. I would like to forecast that culture will become more supportive of Christian values, and thus the life of a priest will become easier. But it seems clear to me that the tsunami of secularization is just beginning to sweep across the world. We are not at the end of this process, we are at the beginning.

I have no idea where society is going or where it will end up. Cardinal George of Chicago said it well, "The world divorced from the God who created and redeemed it inevitably comes to a bad end."[26]

What I can see now is a new cohort of committed Catholic priests and faith-filled laity rising up. They will no longer be part of a dominant religious culture. They will become increasingly a fervent minority. Their values and beliefs will be ever more countercultural. They will be sometimes tolerated, often scorned, occasionally persecuted, and, a few, crucified. This cohort will be a brilliant light in the darkness.

The values and worldview of Christianity are markedly different from those of secularism. Christianity promotes self-giving love, service to others, chastity, and obedience to God's law, including the sanctity of all human life. Secularism, on the other hand, advances sexual "freedom," rejection of "man-made" religious dogmas, and personal self-fulfillment as paramount. The chasm between Christian values and secular society is growing.

For Christianity, God is the author of all and the measure of all. Christianity posits that the human person can only find itself by self-giving to others and God in love. It is Jesus who shows us what it means to be fully human. When humankind rejects God's laws, coded in its very nature, the result is chaos, pain, and eventually human destruction.

For secularism, God is replaced by Man. Man's focus is now on the self. It is now the human person who has become the center. People will no longer serve God; they will serve themselves . . . without God.

Does this sound familiar? It should. This was Satan's choice. He refused to serve God. He would rather rule his own kingdom than serve in God's. The ultimate question for today is this: Who is in charge—God or Man? Remember the first commandment. Ironically, it is precisely in God that human beings find their true fulfillment and their true glory. But, in secularism, this is lost.

I recall an incident when a street preacher, perhaps a little crazy, was preaching aloud to passersby about the need to repent and believe in Jesus as Lord and Savior. Actually, I thought his message was an accurate distillation of the Gospel call to conversion, albeit presented in a disheveled way. A young woman said to him kindly, "Well, that's your truth, but it's not my truth." She was trying to be supportive of the man but clearly thought of herself as outside the Christian dispensation.

However, there can be no "abstaining" from the message of Jesus. One cannot opt out of the Christian call to faith and conversion. In the next life, there are ultimately only two options: heaven and hell. There is no place for those who "opt out." With each choice we make on earth, we, consciously or unconsciously, choose one or the other.

As we choose God and travel down the path to holiness, we become increasingly full of grace and thus mirror the future life of heaven. As we choose love and goodness, we are choosing God, and these increasingly become our life.

However, as one chooses against God, the tragedy of a separation from all things divine must invade one's life. This "hell" is a place of rage, violence, a self-focusing narcissism, isolation, and a desire to destroy all things of God. Sadly, this must be the lot of all those who reject God, either consciously or unconsciously.

As secularism sweeps over many nations, there will be a growing number of people who will disdain Christianity and the divine. We have already seen examples of this. As the scriptures tell us, "No one can serve two masters. He will either hate one and love the other, or be devoted to one and despise the other" (Mt 6:24). Is it any wonder that criticism and rejection of Christian values are on the rise in bastions of secularity?

As the tsunami of secularism sweeps across the world, the rejection of God and the Church will increase. Not only will the criticism continue, it will likely get worse. The subjects may change, but the underlying antipathy will not. My brothers, these letters are an attempt to help prepare us for these difficult days ahead.

As Benedict XVI prophesied:

> And so it seems certain to me that the Church is facing very hard times. The real crisis has scarcely begun. We will have to count on terrific upheavals. But I am equally certain about what will remain at the end: . . . the Church of faith. She may well no longer be the dominant social power to the extent that she was until recently; but she will enjoy a flesh blossoming and be seen as man's home, where he will find life and hope beyond death.[27]

What should we priests do now? How should we respond? I have two suggestions. First, preach and live the Gospel. Like St. Paul, we must preach Jesus. We must speak about his saving death and resurrection. When people embrace the Truth, all else eventually falls into place. Also, we must live it! We must love one another, especially those who hate us. When we love those who reject us, we most surely image our heavenly Father.

Second, trust in God. The battle has already been won. Jesus has definitively triumphed over evil. In fact, each time the Church is excoriated, it emerges even stronger. Each time it walks the path of suffering, it becomes more purified and pours out God's grace even more abundantly. These are days of crucifixion. Thus, they simultaneously become days of brilliant resurrection.

I have told you this so that you might have peace in me. In the world you will have trouble, but take courage, I have conquered the world.

—John 16:33

Notes

1. Tom W. Smith, "Trends in Well-being, 1972–2010," March, 2011, http://www.norc.org/PDFs/publications/GSSTrendsinWellbeing_March2011.pdf.

2. See Stephen J. Rossetti, *Why Priests Are Happy: A Study of the Psychological and Spiritual Health of Priests* (Notre Dame, IN: Ave Maria Press, 2011), 86–89, 96–97.

3. Mick Brown, "Godless in Tumourville: Christopher Hitchens Interview," *Telegraph*, January 31, 2013, http://www.telegraph.co.uk/culture/books/8388695/Godless-in-Tumourville-Christopher-Hitchens-interview.html.

4. Cardinal Seán P. O'Malley, "Pro Life Homily" (Washington, D.C., January 24, 2013), http://www.homilybostoncatholic.org/Utility/News-And-Press/Content.aspx?id=25842.

5. Richard Dawkins, (speech, Reason Rally 2012, March 24, 2012), http://ladydifadden.wordpress.com/

2012/03/28/transcript-of-richard-dawkins-speech-from-reason-rally-2012.

6. Rossetti, *Why Priests Are Happy.*

7. Ibid., 167–76.

8. Ibid., 105–07.

9. Dean C. Ludwig and Clinton O. Longenecker, "The Bathsheba Syndrome: The Ethical Failure of Successful Leaders," *Journal of Business Ethics* 12, no. 4 (April 1993): 265–73.

10. St. Augustine, "From a Sermon on Pastors," in *Liturgy of the Hours,* vol. 4 (New York: Catholic Book Publishing, 1975), 254.

11. Roger Landry, "Revenge of the Black Toad and Miser of Souls," *CatholiCity,* March 5, 2010, http://www.catholicity.com/commentary/landry/00826.html.

12. Ibid.

13. John Stuart Mill, quoted in "Affirm Quotes," *BrainyQuote,* accessed March 22, 2013, http://www.brainyquote.com/quotes/keywords/affirm.html.

14. "Havana Prelate Shares Notes From Cardinal Bergoglio's Pre-Conclave Speech: Argentine Archbishop Warned Against a 'Worldly Church,'" *ZENIT,* March 26, 2013, http://www.zenit.org/en/articles/havana-prelate-shares-notes-from-cardinal-bergoglio-s-pre-conclave-speech.

15. Pope Francis (homily, Chrism Mass, March 28, 2013), http://www.vatican.va/holy_father/francesco/homilies/2013/documents/papa-francesco_20130328_messa-crismale_en.html.

16. "Pope Francis has lunch with Rome priests," *Vatican Radio,* March 30, 2013, http://en.radio-

vaticana.va/news/2013/03/30 pope_francis_
has_lunch_with_rome_priests/en1-678250.

17. Rossetti, *Why Priests Are Happy*, 111.

18. George P. Matysek Jr., "Colbert Report Chaplain Says God Wants Us to Laugh," *The Narthex* (blog), July 30, 2011, https://reviewmatysek.wordpress.com/category/scripture.

19. Sharon Otterman, "New York's Next Cardinal," *New York Times*, January 6, 2012, http://www.nytimes.com/2012/01/08/nyregion/timothy-dolan-new-yorks-next-cardinal.html.

20. Pope Francis (homily, Chrism Mass, March 28, 2013).

21. Pope Francis (*Audience with the College of Cardinals*, March 15, 2013), http://www.vatican.va/holy_father/francesco/speeches/2013/march/documents/papa-francesco_20130315_cardinali_en.html.

22. Pope John Paul II, letter *To Priests*, (Holy Thursday 2004, March 28, 2004), http://www.vatican.va/holy_father/john_paul_ii/letters/2004/documents/hf_jp-ii_let_20040406_priests-holy-thursday_en.html.

23. Kieran Kavanaugh and Otilio Rodriguez, trans., *The Collected Works of St. John of the Cross* (Washington, D.C.: ICS Publications, 1979), 717.

24. Ibid., 712.

25. David Van Biema, "Mother Teresa's Crisis of Faith," *Time*, August 23, 2007, http://www.time.com/time/magazine/article/0,9171,1655720,00.html. See also Mother Teresa and Brian Kolodiejchuk, *Come Be My Light* (New York: Doubleday, 2007).

26. Tim Drake, "The Myth and the Reality of 'I'll Die in My Bed' What Cardinal Francis George Really Said," *National Catholic Register*, October 24,

2012. http://www.ncregister.com/blog/tim-drake/
the-myth-and-the-reality-of-ill-die-in-my-bed.

27. Elizabeth Scalia, "Pope Benedict: Faith and the
Future," *Patheos*, February 12, 2012 http://www.
patheos.com/blogs/theanchoress/2012/02/16/
pope-benedict-faith-and-the-future/.

Msgr. Stephen J. Rossetti, a priest of the Diocese of Syracuse, served for many years at Saint Luke Institute in Silver Spring, Maryland, where he became president and CEO. A priest of the Diocese of Syracuse, he previously served in two diocesan parishes. He is a licensed psychologist with a doctorate in psychology from Boston College and a doctor of ministry from the Catholic University of America. He is the author of scores of articles and several books, including *Born of the Eucharist*, *The Joy of Priesthood*—recipient of a Catholic Press Association book award—and *When the Lion Roars*, and is editor of *Behold Your Mother*.

Rossetti received a Proclaim Award from the USCCB as well as a Lifetime Service Award from the Theological College of the Catholic University of America. In 2010, he received the Touchstone Award from the National Federation of Priests' Councils for a lifetime of work with priests. In 2013, Rossetti received the Pope John Paul II Seminary Leadership Award from NCEA for distinguished service in priestly formation and was awarded a doctor of divinity degree, honoris causa, from St. Mary's Seminary and University in Maryland.

Rossetti lectures to priests and religious internationally on priestly spirituality and wellness issues. He serves as clinical associate professor of pastoral studies at the Catholic University of America and is a visiting professor at Gregorian University in Rome.

Founded in 1865, Ave Maria Press,
a ministry of the Congregation of
Holy Cross, is a Catholic publishing
company that serves the spiritual and
formative needs of the Church and its
schools, institutions, and ministers;
Christian individuals and families; and
others seeking spiritual nourishment.

For a complete listing of titles from

Ave Maria Press

Sorin Books

Forest of Peace

Christian Classics

visit www.avemariapress.com

 ave maria press® / Notre Dame, IN 46556
A Ministry of the United States Province of Holy Cross